KU-775-708

CONTENTS

THE WEIMAR REPUBLIC

STEPHEN J. LEE

Routledge
Taylor & Francis Group

LONDON AND NEW YORK

First published 1998
by Routledge
11 New Fetter Lane, London EC4P 4EE

Simultaneously published in the USA and Canada
by Routledge
29 West 35th Street, New York, NY 10001

Reprinted 2001, 2003

Routledge is an imprint of the Taylor & Francis Group

Typeset in Grotesque and Perpetua by Keystoke
Jacaranda Lodge, Wolverhampton
Printed and bound in Great Britain by
MPG Books Ltd, Bodmin, Cornwall

British Library Cataloguing in Publication Data
A catalogue record for this book is available from the British Library

Library of Congress Cataloging in Publication Data
Lee, Stephen J.
   The Weimar Republic / Stephen J. Lee
      p.   cm. – (Questions and analysis in history)
   Includes bibliographical references and index.
   ISBN 0–415–17178–4
      1. Germany–Politics and government–1918–1933. 2. Germany–
   Social conditions–1918–1933. 3. Germany–Economic conditions.
   4. Germany–Foreign relations–1918–1933. I. Title. II. Series
   DD240.L394 1998
   943.085–dc21   97–39300
                                                              CIP

ISBN 0–415–17178–4

THE WEIMAR
REPUBLIC

QUESTIONS AND ANALYSIS IN HISTORY

Edited by Stephen J. Lee and Sean Lang

Other titles in this series:

Imperial Germany, 1871–1918
Stephen J. Lee

Hitler and Nazi Germany
Stephen J. Lee

The French Revolution
Jocelyn Hunt

Parliamentary Reform 1785–1928
Sean Lang

The Spanish Civil War
Andrew Forrest

SERIES PREFACE

Most history textooks now aim to provide the student with interpretation, and many also cover the historiography of a topic. Some include a selection of sources.

So far, however, there has been no attempt to combine *all* the skills needed by the history student. Interpretation is usually found within an overall narrative framework and it is often difficult to separate out the two for essay purposes. Where sources are included, there is rarely any guidance as to how to answer the questions on them.

The Questions and Analysis series is therefore based on the belief that another approach should be added to those which already exist. It has two main aims.

The first is to separate narrative from interpretation so that the latter is no longer diluted by the former. Each chapter starts with a background narrative section containing essential information. This material is then used in a section focusing on analysis through a specific question. The main purpose of this is to help to tighten up essay technique.

The second aim is to provide a comprehensive range of sources for each of the issues covered. The questions are of the type which appear on examination papers, and some have worked answers to demonstrate the techniques required.

The chapters may be approached in different ways. The background narratives can be read first to provide an overall perspective, followed by the analyses and then the sources. The alternative method is to work through all the components of each chapter before going on to the next.

ACKNOWLEDGEMENTS

Author and publisher are grateful to the following for permission to reproduce copyright material.

For written sources: V.R. Berghahn, *Modern Germany: Society, Economy and Politics in the Twentieth Century* (Cambridge University Press, first published 1982, edition used, 1995); J.A.S. Grenville, *The Major International Treaties, 1914–1973* (Methuen, 1974); A. Kaes, M. Jay and E. Dimendberg, (eds) *The Weimar Republic Sourcebook* (University of California Press, Berkeley, 1994); J.W. Hiden, *The Weimar Republic* (Longman, 1974); J. Laver, *Imperial and Weimar Germany* (Hodder & Stoughton, 1992); G. Layton, *From Bismarck to Hitler: Germany 1890–1933* (Hodder & Stoughton, 1995); J. Noakes and G. Pridham, *Nazism, 1919–1945* (University of Exeter Press, 1996 edition); J.J.K. Peukert, *The Weimar Republic* (Penguin Books, trans, 1991); J. Remak (ed.) *The Nazi Years* (Prentice-Hall, Englewood Cliffs, N.J., 1969); L.L. Snyder, *The Weimar Republic* (Van Nostrand, Princeton N.J., 1996); *The German White Book Concerning the Responsibility of the Authors of the War* (New York, 1924); Count Max Montéglas, *The Case for the Central Powers* (London, 1925); Philip Scheidemann, *The Making of New Germany: Memoirs*, trans. J.E. Michell II (Appleton Century Crofts, Inc., New York, 1929); W.G. Runciman (ed.) *Max Weber, Selections in Translation*, trans. E. Matthews (Cambridge University Press, 1978); Alma Luckau, *The German Delegation at the Paris Peace Conference* (Columbia University Press, New York, 1941); Harlan R. Crippen (ed.) *Germany: A Self Portrait* (Oxford University Press, London, 1944); G. Bry, *Wages in Germany, 1871–1945* (Princeton University Press, 1960); F.K. Ringer (ed.) *The German Inflation of 1923* (Oxford University Press, 1969); Eric Sutton (ed. and trans.) *Gustav Stresemann: His Diaries, Letters and Papers*, II, 1935–7 (The Macmillan Company and Curtis Brown Ltd., New York); *The League of Nations Official Journal*, special supplement no. 44.

For illustrations used, acknowledgements are due to the following: AKG London; Hoover Institution Archives; Bilderdienst Süddeutscher Verlag; Wiener Library; and Akademie der Kunste.

1

THE GERMAN REVOLUTION, 1918–19

BACKGROUND NARRATIVE

Germany was taken into the First World War in August 1914 by a
civilian government under Bethmann Hollweg, the fifth Chancellor
of the Second Reich. By July 1917 his regime had been converted
into a military dictatorship under Field Marshals Ludendorff and
Hindenburg. This, however, made little difference to Germany's
prospects in the war. Despite defeating Russia in the East, the Reich
faced imminent collapse in the West by October 1918. The decisive
factors were the entry of the United States into the war and a
crippling blockade imposed by the Royal Navy. Ludendorff therefore advised Kaiser Wilhelm II to appoint a civilian government
to negotiate an armistice with the Allies. Prince Max of Baden
was entrusted with this unenviable task on 26 October. He was
supported by the Social Democrats (SPD), who since 1912 had been
the largest party in the Reichstag, but opposed by the more radical
Independent Socialists (USPD) and Spartacists, who had broken
away from the SPD during the course of the war.

The situation then deteriorated rapidly as the armed forces
began to disintegrate. The result was a series of mutinies. On 7
November Bavaria also erupted when the Wittelsbach dynasty was
overthrown, to be replaced by an Independent Socialist regime
under Eisner. The Kaiser was persuaded to abdicate on 9 November.
On the same day, Prince Max of Baden handed over the reins of

government to Friedrich Ebert, who succeeded him as Chancellor, while the latter's SPD colleague, Philipp Scheidemann, proclaimed Germany a Republic from a window in the Reichstag building.

At this stage the SPD were obliged to share power with the radicals – the USPD and Spartacists – in a Council of People's Representatives. It was no secret, however, that the groups had vastly different aims. The SPD hoped to establish a western parliamentary system, while the Spartacist leaders, Karl Liebknecht and Rosa Luxemburg, clearly intended to emulate the Bolshevik Revolution in Russia. In January 1919, the Spartacists came out in open revolt in the streets of Berlin. They were, however, crushed by the Freikorps, or remnants of the Imperial army, with the full knowledge and sanction of Ebert, who had already done a deal with the commanding officer, General Groener. During the fighting both Liebknecht and Luxemburg were shot in cold blood. The next target was Bavaria, which had proclaimed a Soviet Republic in January. This regime was brought down by the Freikorps in April 1919.

Meanwhile, elections had been held for the convening of the first full assembly of the Republic. This met in Weimar but, once the violence in Berlin had ended, the legislature was transferred back to Berlin, which once again became the permanent capital.

ANALYSIS: WAS THERE A GERMAN REVOLUTION?

'Revolution' involves the transfer of power in circumstances outside of the normal constitutional process. It results in radical changes to the political – and quite possibly social and economic – infrastructure. The process is usually accelerated by the experience of war, and especially of military defeat. This is what happened in Russia during the course of 1917.

There has always been a strong argument that Germany had a similar experience a year later. The usual interpretation is that, like Russia, Germany underwent either two revolutions, or a single revolution which developed in two stages. A 'revolution from above' liberalised the constitution of the Second Reich in October 1918. It was followed by a 'revolution from below', which further subdivided into two. One successfully laid the foundations of the Republic in November and then beat off attempts to establish a more radical

Bolshevik-style regime in January 1919. Collectively these developments comprised the 'German Revolution', which transformed an authoritarian structure into an advanced democracy. This scenario can – and should – be challenged. It will be argued here that Germany certainly did experience a revolutionary situation in 1918 but that it is far from clear that this situation actually produced a revolution.

'Revolution from above', it has been argued, was initiated at the end of September 1918 by Ludendorff and the Army High Command or OHL (*Oberste Heeresleitung*). Recognising that Germany's defeat was imminent, they advised the Kaiser to hand over power to Prince Max of Baden in an attempt to secure a constitutional government which would be acceptable to the Allies in general and to President Wilson in particular. The 'revolution' was activated by the reforms of 28 October which for the first time made the Chancellor responsible to the Reichstag and enabled members within the Reichstag to become ministers. The constitutional base of the Second Reich was therefore completely transformed.

The underlying situation was certainly dramatic. Germany faced military disaster and two of her allies, Bulgaria and Austria-Hungary, had already collapsed. The First World War was therefore the agent for political change, just as the Franco-Prussian War had been in 1871. Then, the Second Reich had been born out of military victory, based on the absorption of Germany into Prussia under the personal hegemony of the Hohenzollerns. Now, that same regime was being transformed by the spectre of military defeat. Ironically, the last country to have made an equivalent transition as a direct result of war was Germany's victim of 1870: France had changed from the Second Empire into the Third Republic. There is, it seems, much to be said for Trotsky's maxim that 'war is the locomotive of history'.

But did a revolutionary situation actually produce a *revolution*? The political and constitutional developments of October 1918 were all predictable. There had been persistent pressure for such changes throughout the history of the Second Reich by the Progressives, Social Democrats, National Liberals and even the Centre Party. The concessions were therefore very much within the mainstream reform programme of all the progressive elements of the regime. What occurred in September 1918 was not a sudden and radical departure but rather the fulfilment of a long awaited objective. 'Revolution from above' is a less appropriate description of this process than, say, evolution accelerated by necessity.

There is a stronger case for saying that November's 'revolution from below' was a real one. All the constituents seemed to be present. First, the military crisis destabilised the new administration of Prince Max, who was compelled to give up after only six weeks. Second, ever increasing pressure was exerted from outside Germany as President Wilson demanded unconditional surrender. Third, this precipitated action from below. As an awareness of the desperate nature of the situation spread through Germany there was a strong pressure for the abdication of the Kaiser and other German rulers. The wave of unrest was sparked off by the naval mutinies at Wilhelmshaven, Kiel, Hamburg, Bremen and Lübeck and by army disaffection in Frankfurt, Cologne, Stuttgart and Leipzig. There was undeniably a popular momentum which proved irresistible and which swept away the constitutional compromise implicit in the government of Prince Max. Fourth, the arrangement which followed seemed to be far more radical than the earlier October reforms. Scheidemann's proclamation of the Republic on 9 November was followed, a day later, by the formation of the Council of People's Representatives (*Rat der Volksbeauftragten*) comprising Ebert, Scheidemann and Landsberg from the SPD and Haase, Dittman and Barth from the USPD. Similar institutions were set up in all the German states following the abdication of their rulers. Could these not be seen as revolutionary institutions?

Not necessarily. Despite the chaos of November 1917 and the undeniable potential for revolution, there is again strong evidence that the transfer of power was evolutionary. When Prince Max handed over to Ebert on 9 November 1918 he said, 'I commend the German Reich to your care.' (1) It was never Ebert's intention to bring any fundamental political changes. He hoped instead to reconstruct an administration on the basis of the October reforms and to form a caretaker government which would include the SPD, the USPD, the Centre and the Progressives, until a national assembly could be called to decide upon a future constitution. To an extent his hand was forced. Ebert found Scheidemann's proclamation of the Republic on 9 November profoundly irritating; he said on the occasion: 'You have no right to proclaim the Republic. What becomes of Germany – whether she becomes a republic or something else – must be decided by a constituent assembly.' (2) The possibility of power going to the soldiers' and workers' councils meant that Ebert felt obliged to go along with the apparently revolutionary device of the Council of People's Representatives instead of his own preferred option. Nevertheless, he did whatever he could to prevent this from pursuing a radical path and to pull the whole process back on to the course he had originally envisaged.

The whole attitude of Ebert fits into the pattern of recent developments within the SPD which had actually made them a force for stability and continuity. Even before 1900 the party had been engaged in active debate between the 'revolutionary' minority and the 'evolutionary' mainstream led by Bernstein. The radicals had broken away during the First World War to form the USPD and Spartacus League, the latter espousing Marxist-Leninist principles. The majority Social Democrats now showed no enthusiasm for anything other than a reformed version of the constitution of the Second Reich. Some historians have argued that they dismissed the alternatives too lightly; according to Wehler, for example, workers' and soldiers' councils 'could have been used to restructure society, if the political leadership of the time had encouraged such a course with more determination than it showed'. (3) Bookbinder agrees: the Social Democrats were so preoccupied with preventing political revolution that they lost the chance to seek social change. This, in turn, 'convinced the conservatives that they could limit any concessions that they might make.' (4) It would therefore be difficult to argue even that the Social Democrats were 'reluctant revolutionaries'; on the contrary, twenty years of internal debate had made them convinced evolutionaries, prepared to take any measure necessary to prevent revolution. This became more and more apparent at the end of 1918 and the beginning of 1919. The situation again seemed highly volatile as the Social Democrats, in alliance with the military, took action to prevent a Bolshevik-style *coup* by the Spartacists. Some historians, like Erdmann, maintain that this was necessary to maintain the liberal-democratic course, which had been started in November 1918, from the threat of totalitarian dictatorship from the left. Marxist-Leninist historians, by contrast, claim that a genuine mass movement, led by Luxemburg and Liebknecht, was betrayed by the Social Democrats in collusion with the forces of reaction. Different though they are in other respects, these two interpretations agree on the revolutionary nature of the Spartacist initiative.

On the surface, there is much to support such an approach. It reflects the two very different perceptions of progress which had grown out of the SPD. One was trying to defend the liberal-democratic achievement against the Communist threat, while the other was seeking to accelerate the movement towards socialism. The Spartacists wanted close association between Germany and Soviet Russia, together with a transfer of all political power to the workers' and soldiers' councils, the establishment of a workers' militia, collectivisation of larger agricultural units and the nationalisation of many industries. This explains why the SPD were so quick to abandon the workers' and soldiers' councils as a representative device, seeing in them a direct influence of the Russian system of soviets of workers' and soldiers' deputies. Instead, the SPD leadership were prepared to take a pragmatic course by making a deal with Groener and the Freikorps.

No one could reasonably argue that the Social Democrats were not genuinely acting to prevent revolution in December 1918 and January 1919. But it is possible that they greatly exaggerated the danger and therefore swung too readily into a counter-revolutionary position to prevent a revolution which was not really happening; this, in turn, helped determine the essentially conservative nature of the Weimar Republic.

Recent research by German historians such as Kolb, Feldman and Kluge has shown that the Spartacists did not have the previously assumed control over the workers' and soldiers' councils. Nor, indeed, were these councils incompatible with the concept of constitutional democracy: indeed, Kolb maintains that 'the great majority of the former were dominated by Majority Socialists and moderate independents, while in the soldiers' councils not only Social Democrats but also bourgeois elements exercised considerable influence.' (5) According to Berghahn, 'the objectives of the overwhelming majority of the Councils were also moderate, comprising no more than the traditional catalogue of demands of mainstream Social democracy.' (6) The Spartacists were, by contrast, in control of relatively few councils. The councils cannot therefore be seen as the nucleus of a revolutionary alternative to moderate constitutionalism.

Nor were the Spartacists ready for revolution. Recent historians have pointed to the movement's almost complete lack of organisation: Kolb, for example, maintains that it was 'without a clear strategic plan, was hopelessly mismanaged and to some extent half-hearted'. (7) There was no equivalent to the precision of the Bolshevik takeover in Petrograd and Moscow a year earlier. Luxemburg and Liebknecht did not even believe that the time was right for an insurrection but were drawn into a situation which was uncontrolled and chaotic. They paid with their lives.

In the circumstances the reaction of the SPD was tougher than it need have been. It would be inappropriate to take the Marxist view that Ebert's government simply crushed by counter-revolution any achievements that had been made in November 1918. But it is arguable that Ebert stopped well short of the sort of reforms which the government might have accomplished if it had been prepared to take as tough a line with the establishment as with the radical left. In the event, the Republic as constituted – and defended – by Ebert's government contained many residual influences and structures from the Second

Reich. Hiden goes so far as to say: 'That great violence was also used against the German communists was a sad and bitter comment on the nature of the relationship developing between Ebert and the German establishment. In that sense, at least, the Weimar Republic may be called the last act of Empire.' (8)

There are four main examples of this continuity between Republic and Reich. First, the constitution, which was eventually adopted in July 1919, was essentially a compromise: the base was the previous constitution, modified by the October reforms and given a republican superstructure. Article 1 even affirms: 'The German Reich is a Republic.' (9) Second, the adaptation was relatively straightforward for the moderate political parties who comprised most of the earlier coalition governments. The SPD and Centre (Z) made the transition virtually unchanged, while the Progressives and National Liberals were little modified as the Democrats (DDP) and People's Party (DVP) respectively. It was a case of the constitutional opposition to the Kaiser's administration now inheriting the right to become that administration, but this implies constitutional evolution rather than political revolution. Third, there was no attempt to make structural changes to the judiciary or the civil service. As will be seen in the next chapter, these became powerful forces for conservatism and weighted the operation of the law heavily in favour of the right and against the left. Above all, the Republican government was careful not to interfere in the attempts of the army to revive itself after the catastrophe of defeat. The military rump, limited by the Treaty of Versailles (1919) to 100,000 volunteers, became a highly professional core based very much on the ethos of the Second Reich. The decision not to republicanise the military really stemmed from Ebert's telephone conversation with Groener on 9 November. Hence, as Heiber maintains, 'The entire old apparatus and its incumbents were allowed to go on operating without let or hindrance, at first provisionally, but later with the republican constitution ultimately removing all their worries.' (10)

We are therefore left with a paradox. Germany in 1918 had all the ingredients necessary for revolution: defeat in war, a disintegrating army and a radicalised left. And yet there was a surprising degree of continuity within Germany's transition from Empire to Republic. Apparently desperate situations were relieved by pragmatic decisions which prevented radical changes. Hiden argues that the Revolution was 'the link between the former German Empire and the Weimar Republic'. (11) It would perhaps make more sense to reverse the metaphor and see the link between the Empire and Republic preventing revolution. The year 1918, in short, saw in Germany a revolutionary situation but without a revolution. Or, put another way, if there was a revolution, it did not revolutionise.

Questions

1. Which argument do you find more convincing: there was or there was not a revolution in Germany in 1918–19?
2. Why did the Social Democrats, and not the Spartacists, shape the new Republic in 1918 and 1919?
3. Why is the question as to whether there was a revolution significant for the future development of the Weimar Republic? (You may wish to return to this after having completed the rest of the topics.)

SOURCES

1. CONTEMPORARY VIEWS OF THE REVOLUTION

Source A: from an article by Friedrich Meinecke in *Deutsche Allgemeine Zeitung*, 20 November 1918.

Our constitutional reform was possible in the fashion in which it transpired due to the pressure of the international situation, for which the old system was no longer fit. But that elements very capable of development, forward pointing, and ready for reform already existed in our now-bygone ancien regime is demonstrated by the fact that the constitutional transformation – the substance of which represents an enormous revolution – despite its abruptness, was completed with astounding calm, carried by the judgement and unanimity of all legislative elements. It therefore fell into the laps of the people like an overripe fruit.

Source B: from Kurt Tucholsky's *Wir Negativen*, 13 March 1919.

If revolution means merely collapse, then it was one; but no one should expect the ruins to look any different from the old building. We have suffered failure and hunger, and those responsible just walked away. And the people remain: they had their old flags torn down, but had no new ones ... We confront a Germany full of unrivalled corruption, full of profiteers and sneaks, full of three hundred thousand devils among whom each assumes the right to secure his black self from the effects of revolution ... We have the opportunity of choice: do we fight ... with love or do we fight ... with hate? We want to fight with hate out of love. With hate against that fellow who has dared to drink the blood of his countrymen . . . with hate against the clique to which the disproportionate snatching up of property and the misery of cottage workers appears to be the will of God . . . We fight in any case with hate. But we fight out of love for the oppressed.

Source C: from the reminiscences of Bernhard Prince von Bülow, published in 1931.

In Berlin on November 9, I witnessed the beginnings of revolution. Alas, she did not come . . . in the shape of a radiant goddess, her hair flowing in the wind, and shod with sandals of iron. She was like an old hag, toothless and bald, her great feet slipshod and down at the heel. The German revolution was drearily philistine, lacking in all fire or inspiration . . . Our new masters were . . . unfit to govern. Most characteristic of their mentality was the speech from the Reichstag steps, delivered by Scheidemann . . . who, in proclaiming the Republic, began his oration with the following: 'The German people have won all along the line.' A stupid lie! And a very cruel piece of self-deception! No, alas, the German people had not 'won' – it had been conquered, overpowered by a host of enemies, wretchedly misled politically, reduced by famine, and stabbed in the back!

To any unbiased spectator of these events, to whoever watched it all in the one hope that the German nation might not perish, these first days of our republic were days of the return to chaos. Children could scarcely have done worse.

Questions

1. What was the Reichstag (Source C)? [1]
   Who was Scheidemann (Source C)? [1]
*2. How do Sources A, B and C differ in their interpretation of the 1918 Revolution? How would you explain these differences? [6]
3. Compare the reliability of Sources A, B and C to the historian studying the origins of the Weimar Republic. [6]
4. How effectively do the authors of Sources A, B, and C make use of language to emphasise their message? [4]
5. Using the three sources and your own knowledge, comment on the view that there was no revolution in November 1918. [7]

Worked answer

*2. [Both parts of the question need to be addressed fully. In an examination paper they might even be asked separately. There should be an introductory sentence, followed by two paragraphs. The first could focus on the contrasts between the sources themselves, using selected examples. The second needs reference to the context of the sources and the speakers. This requires some inferences and a little background knowledge.]

The Sources provide very different analyses, representing the centre, far left and right of the political spectrum.

Meinecke (Source A) emphasised the positive nature of effortless change in the form of continuity with the past; this was because the 'bygone ancien regime' contained all the necessary potential for reform which had now been 'completed with astounding calm'. To Tucholsky (Source B), on the other hand, any change from the former system was entirely negative: any revolution there might have been had collapsed, since 'those responsible just walked away'. The result was exploitation, 'unrivalled corruption' and widespread selfishness. Von Bülow (Source C) shared the disillusionment of Tucholsky, referring to a 'return to chaos', but he used a different perspective. The Revolution was caused by conquest 'by a host of enemies', and by the army being 'stabbed in the back'.

The differences between these attitudes can be explained by the political standpoints of their authors. Meinecke was a historian: he was therefore likely to see links with the past. As a liberal and a supporter of the new Republic, his main fear was that the arrival of democracy had been so easy that it might now be undervalued. Tucholsky, by contrast, was of the radical left. He therefore rejected the achievement of liberal democracy, welcomed by Meinecke, and anticipated further conflict on behalf of 'the oppressed'. Von Bülow's views were typical of those of the conservative right and, because of the time lapse before publication in 1931, had been influenced by the 'stab in the back' myth. Like the rest of the right, he considered the Republic to have been tainted by its origins.

SOURCES

2. THE BIRTH OF THE REPUBLIC – AND ITS ENEMIES

Source D: from Philip Scheidemann's *The Making of the New Germany: Memoirs* (1929).

On the morning of 9th November, 1918, the Reichstag was like an armed camp. Working men and soldiers were going in and out.

... Then a crowd of workers and soldiers rushed into the hall and made straight for our table.

Fifty of them yelled out at the same time, 'Scheidemann, come along with us at once Philipp, you must come out and speak.'

I refused: how many times had I not already spoken!

'You must, you must, if trouble is to be avoided. There are thousands upon thousands outside shouting for you to speak. Come along quick, Scheidemann! Liebknecht is already speaking from the balcony of the Schloss'... 'Liebknecht intends to proclaim the Soviet Republic!'

... There was no doubt at all. The man who could bring along the 'Bolshies' from the Schloss to the Reichstag or the Social Democrats from the Reichstag to the Schloss had won the day.

I saw the Russian folly staring me in the face – the Bolshevist tyranny, the substitute for the tyranny of the Czars! No, no, Germany should not have that on the top of all her other miseries.

... I was already standing at the window... The shouts of the crowds sounded like a mighty chorus. Then there was silence. I only said a few words, which were received with tremendous cheering.

'Workers and soldiers, frightful were those four years of war, ghastly the sacrifices of the people made in blood and treasure. The cursed War is at an end... The Emperor has abdicated. He and his friends have decamped. The people have triumphed over them all along the line. Prince Max of Baden has handed over his office as Chancellor to Ebert. Our friend will form a Labour Government to which all Socialist Parties will belong...

'... Workmen and soldiers, realize the historic importance of today. Miracles have happened. Long and incessant toil is before us. Everything for the people; everything by the people! Nothing must be done that brings dishonour to the Labour movement. Stand united and loyal, and be conscious of your duty. The old and rotten – the monarchy – has broken down. Long live the new! Long live the German Republic!'

Source E: from the Spartacus Manifesto, 26 November 1918.

PROLETARIANS! MEN AND WOMEN OF LABOUR! COMRADES!

The revolution has made its entry into Germany. The masses of soldiers, who for four years were driven to the slaughterhouse for the sake of capitalist profits, and the masses of workers, who for four years were exploited, crushed and starved, have revolted . . . That fearful tool of oppression – Prussian militarism, that scourge of humanity – lies broken on the ground. Its most noticeable representatives, and therewith the most noticeable of those guilty of this war, the Kaiser and the Crown Prince, have fled from the country. Workers' and soldiers' councils have been formed everywhere.

Proletarians of all countries, we do not say that in Germany all the power has really been lodged in the hands of the working people, that the complete triumph of the proletarian revolution has already been attained. There still sit in the government all those socialists who in August 1914 abandoned our most precious possession, the International, who for four years betrayed the German working class and at the same time the International.

But, proletarians of all countries, now the German proletarians are speaking to you. We believe we have the right to appeal before your forum in their name. From the first day of this war we endeavoured to do our international duty by fighting that criminal government with all our power . . .

. . . Proletarians of all countries, when we now summon you to a common struggle, it is not done for the sake of the German capitalists who, under the label of 'German nation', are trying to escape the consequences of their own crime; it is being done for our sake as well as yours. Remember that your victorious capitalists stand ready to suppress in blood our revolution, which they fear as their own. You yourselves have not become any freer through the 'victory', you have only become more enslaved . . .

. . . Therefore the proletariat of Germany is looking toward you in this hour. Germany is pregnant with the social revolution, but socialism can be realized only by the proletariat of the world.

Source F: Rosa Luxemburg: *The Founding Manifesto of the Communist Party*, 31 December 1918.

The question today is not democracy or dictatorship. The question that history has put on the agenda reads: bourgeois democracy or socialist democracy. For dictatorship of the proletariat is democracy in the socialist sense of the word. Dictatorship of the proletariat does not mean bombs, putsches, riots and anarchy, as the agents of capitalist profits deliberately and falsely claim. Rather it means using all instruments of political power to achieve socialism, to expropriate the capitalist class, through and in accordance with the will of the revolutionary majority of the proletariat.

Source G: from an article in *Vorwärts*, a newspaper of the SPD, 24 December 1918.

It was hunger that forced the Russian people under the yoke of militarism ... Bolshevik militarism is the violent despotism of a clique, the dictatorship of the idlers and those unwilling to work. Russia's army, made up of masses of unemployed workers, is today already waging another bloody war.
Let the Russian example be a warning. Do we also want another war? Do we want terror, the bloody reign of a caste?
NO!
We want no more bloodshed and no militarism. We want to achieve peace through work. We want peace, in order not to degenerate into a militarism dictated by the unemployed, as in Russia. Bolshevik bums call the armed masses into the streets, and armed masses, bent on violence, are militarism personified. But we do not want militarism of the right or of the left.
Bolshevism, the lazy man's militarism, knows no freedom or equality. It is vandalism and terror by a small group that arrogates power. So do not follow Spartacus, the German Bolsheviks, unless you want to ruin our economy and trade.
The collapse of German industry and trade means the downfall of the German people.
So, no to terror, not to militaristic rule by loafers and deserters.
Not militarism, but freedom!

Questions

1. Explain the references to Liebknecht (Source D) and Spartacus (Source E). [2]
*2. What considerations should a historian have in mind when assessing the value of Source D as evidence for the origins of the Republic? [6]
3. Does Source D prove that the formation of the Weimar Republic was a 'revolution'? [4]
4. To what extent do Sources E and F complement each other? [5]
5. Using Sources D to F, and your own knowledge, how great a threat did Communism pose to the newly formed republic? [8]

Worked example

*2. [At first sight it seems possible to provide only a short answer to this question. This is deceptive. The analysis needs to be balanced, containing references to both its strengths and weaknesses and to include references to the text and to additional knowledge. It would also be relevant to include a reference to the need for supplementary sources.]

The historian should bear in mind that this source will have both strengths and deficiencies, and that the latter will need to be offset by the use of additional sources.

The strengths are considerable. Scheidemann's description points to the state of confusion which existed, with the Reichstag like 'an armed camp' and 'working men and soldiers' going 'in and out'. It shows that Scheidemann was not intending to speak, but was responding to persuasion: 'Philipp, you must come out . . . ' It confirms the fear of 'the Russian folly' and 'Bolshevist tyranny' and Scheidemann's view that instant action was necessary to prevent Liebknecht from taking power. And, of course, it contains the text of the speech given by Scheidemann from the Reichstag window. Overall, it carries considerable authority: after all, its author became the Republic's second Chancellor.

On the other hand, there are several possible shortcomings. As a personal account, it is likely to be highly subjective, and the lapse of 10 years before its publication in the form of memoirs could have led Scheidemann to over-dramatise the events. How serious was the threat from the Schloss on that same day? Did Scheidemann exaggerate the impact of Liebknecht – or was he simply panicked into making a speech and using the threat of the left as subsequent justification? To answer these questions the historian would need to cross-check with other types of source such as the reports of German and foreign journalists and any photographs or film taken inside and outside the Reichstag building.

2

THE CONSTITUTION
AND POLITICAL SYSTEM

BACKGROUND NARRATIVE

The Constitution of the Weimar Republic was drawn up in January 1919 and submitted to the National Assembly in Weimar in February. Following extensive debate, the constitution was eventually promulgated on 11 August 1919. It contained 181 Articles, grouped into two chapters: the 'Structure and Functions of the Reich' and the 'Fundamental Rights and Duties of the Germans'. The Constitution was regarded by those who framed it as the most advanced in existence at the time.

Meanwhile, over 30 parties contested the elections. The political spectrum was extremely wide. From far left to far right, the main parties were the Communists (KPD), Independent Socialists (SPD), Democrats (DDP), Centre (Z), People's Party (DVP), National Party (DNVP) and Nazis (NSDAP). Most of the governments of the Republic were drawn from members of the SPD, DDP, Centre and DVP. All the governments between 1919 and 1931 were coalitions: these usually comprised the SPD, DDP and Centre. There were, however, alternative combinations, in particular the inclusion of the DVP between 1923 and 1929 and the withdrawal of the SPD for much of the 1920s. Between the declaration of the Republic in November 1918 and the appointment of Hitler in January 1933 there were altogether 16 Chancellors (see list overleaf).

1918–19	Ebert (SPD)
1919	Scheidemann (SPD)
1919–20	Bauer (SPD)
1920	Müller (SPD)
1920–21	Fehrenbach (Z)
1921–22	Wirth (Z)
1922–23	Cuno (non-party)
1923	Stresemann (DVP)
1923–25	Marx (Z)
1925–26	Luther (non-party)
1926	Marx (Z)
1928–30	Muller (SPD)
1930–32	Brüning (Z)
1932	Papen (non-party)
1932–33	Schleicher (non-party)
1933	Hitler

Over the same period there were two Presidents: the SPD leader Ebert from 1919 until 1925 and Hindenburg, not attached to a party although conservative in his views, who was elected in 1925 and re-elected in 1932.

The Republic ran into difficulties under the impact of the Depression from 1929. Müller and the SPD withdrew from the coalition in 1930, leaving a minority cabinet comprising mainly Centre Party ministers. The new Chancellor, Brüning, lacked the necessary majority in the Reichstag and became increasingly dependent on the use of the President's emergency powers under Article 48 of the Constitution. In 1932 the Republic slid towards authoritarian dictatorship as two Chancellors in succession, Papen and Schleicher, governed without a party base at all, bypassing the Reichstag by intensifying the use of presidential decrees. It was in this atmosphere that Hitler was appointed Chancellor in January 1933.

ANALYSIS (1): HOW DEMOCRATIC WAS THE WEIMAR REPUBLIC?

The constitution and political system of the Weimar Republic reveal a major contradiction between theory and practice. In theory they comprised the most advanced democracy in Europe, enshrining a wide range of liberal principles while retaining a degree of stability and continuity with the past. In practice, however, the relationship between the individual components of the constitution was fundamentally flawed. The result was that what started out as a parliamentary regime was captured by the conservative right and converted into an authoritarian one.

The theoretical framework of the Weimar constitution was impeccably democratic. The document, drafted by the liberal jurist Hugo Preuss, aimed to combine the principles of the first Ten Amendments of the Constitution of the United States, the French Declaration of the Rights of Man, and twentieth-century refinements. Hence, by Article 1, 'Political authority emanates from the people'. (1) The electoral system was as advanced as anywhere in Europe, based on 'universal, equal, direct, and secret suffrage by men and women over twenty years of age, according to the principle of proportional representation'. (2) It was heavily influenced by Belgian and Dutch methods, which related the number of votes cast to the size of party representation in parliament; in Germany, this meant one Reichstag seat for every 60,000 votes cast in the country at large. The result was that smaller groups could be included alongside the major parties, allowing for the representation of all interests, whether class, religious, local or sectional. The electorate also had plebiscitary powers, electing every 7 years the President who, as befitted a republican constitution, replaced the former Kaiser as head of state.

A crucial component of a democratic system is the sovereignty of parliament, or the ultimate responsibility of the executive to the legislature. Article 54 of the Weimar Constitution stipulated that 'The Reich Chancellor and the Reich Ministers require for the exercise of their office the confidence of the Reichstag'; (3) this was in complete contrast to the administrations of the former Second Reich. Some democratic systems also include provision for rights of individual states in order to counterbalance the central power with federalism. Section IV of the Constitution guaranteed the autonomy of the German Länder and for the representation of their interests in the Reichsrat. Provision was also made to reduce the traditional power of Prussia which had had the majority of the votes in the old Bundesrat. The population as a whole was guaranteed certain basic rights, including equality before the law (Article 109), 'liberty of travel and residence' (Article 114), the inviolability of the home (Article 115) and the right of every German 'to express his opinion freely by word, in writing, in print, in picture form, or in any other way' (Article 118). Finally, there was even a device, in

---

Article 48, to safeguard democracy by the use of emergency presidential powers should these be necessary. The Reichstag could, however, rescind these if it considered that the President's action was arbitrary.

It seemed therefore that every means had been taken within the Weimar Constitution to promote and defend democracy. Yet in practice there were serious limitations to its operation. Many of the provisions were inherently flawed and were used in ways which were not originally foreseen. There were also knock-on effects as the deficiencies of one component could be offset only by excessive use of another. The result was the reverse of what had been intended – an *imbalance* of powers.

The most chronic of the problems was trying to convert proportional representation into stable government. With 30 or more parties contesting each election, and no national threshold to eliminate the smallest of them, coalition governments quickly became a 'fact of life'. The implications were serious. According to Bookbinder: 'The problems of putting disparate parties with no history of co-operation together and getting them to make significant compromises for the common interest plagued Republican leaders unremittingly.' (4) At first there was a degree of compromise. The three parties most responsible for the Republic, the SPD, DDP and Centre, earned in the 1919 election 76% of the vote which translated into 78% of the seats. But in the election of 1920 their support dropped to only 48% of the vote which meant that the government became dependent on other parties as well. The solution was the support of Stresemann who brought in part of the DVP. Unfortunately, this was offset by the withdrawal between 1923 and 1928 of the SPD. It even became necessary to bring into two cabinets several right-wing politicians from the DNVP. This meant that the base of the government was broadening all the time which made any concerted decision making more difficult. The Depression converted this problem into a crisis as the Chancellor, Müller, withdrew the SPD from the coalition in protest against proposals to cut unemployment benefit. Brüning was left to try to govern Germany with little more than the support of the Centre Party.

It was at this point that the feature of the Constitution intended to safeguard democracy came to be used in a profoundly undemocratic way. The problem experienced by the Chancellor in getting the support of the Reichstag for normal legislation gave enormously enhanced significance to the presidential power. Article 48 enabled him to suspend the normal constitutional processes and govern by decree. As President between 1919 and 1925, Ebert had used this, as intended, only occasionally – as, for example, when the very existence of the Republic was threatened by the Kapp Putsch in 1920. Ebert's successor, Hindenburg, had no compunction about regularising the extraordinary. Entirely unsympathetic to the democratic processes, he used the political embarrassment of Brüning as a means to reduce the power of the Reichstag. He went even further, replacing Brüning in 1932 first with Papen, then with Schleicher, two Chancellors who did not even pretend to have any party support in the Reichstag. After 1931, therefore, presidential authoritarianism almost completely replaced parliamentary sovereignty: Article 48 of the Constitution had swelled in importance, while Article 54 had diminished. The use of decree laws increased from 5 in 1930 to 44 in 1931 and 60 in 1932, while sittings of the Reichstag declined from 94 in 1930 to 41 in 1931 and 13 in 1932. (5) German historians are agreed about the deadly effect of Article 48 in the hands of Hindenburg. According to Eyck: 'his election as president of Germany was a triumph of nationalism and militarism and a heavy defeat for the Republic and parliamentary government.' (6) In Heiber's words, 'It cannot be said that it was a good thing for that state when, after only five years, a dyed-in-the-wool monarchist . . . was invited to occupy its supreme office'. (7) According to Bracher, the eventual outcome of the 'suspension of the Reichstag' and the 'authoritarian experiments of Papen and Schleicher' was 'the terrorist power grab of a minority government under Hitler'. (8)

The internal imbalances within the Weimar Constitution, which eventually enabled the likes of Hindenburg to distort its operation, were accentuated by external pressures, the most important of which was the prevalence of right-wing influences throughout the period of the Republic. There were several manifestations of this, showing increasing co-operation between the conservative right and the radical, or revolutionary, right.

One was the refuge taken by right-wing extremists within *Länder*, like Bavaria, which had conservative administrations. Thus Munich acted as the greenhouse of the Nazi movement. It is true that the Bavarian administration took action to deal with Hitler's putsch in 1923, but the perpetrators were dealt with exceptionally leniently. The judiciary played an important part in this, discriminating all too obviously in favour of right-wing defendants who appeared in the courts while dealing harshly with known leftists. Meanwhile, the traditional core of the army, which controlled the new Reichswehr, sowed distrust of the Republic, using the 'stab in the back' myth to its advantage. The Reichswehr backed Hindenburg's presidential dictatorship after 1931, while individual military men such as Schleicher transferred the political functions of the Chancellorship outside the arena of the Reichstag. Finally, administrative continuity was maintained by the civil service, the composition of which had scarcely changed since the days of the Second Reich and which, in the words of Broszat 'had been unable to reconcile with the party state of the Weimar Republic their traditional conception of the "servant of the state" as the guardian and representative of a disciplined society'. (9) There was therefore a willingness to co-operate with the authoritarian governments after 1930 which had often been missing in the heyday of the Republic. The conservative components were all prepared to risk a transfer of power to the radical right in January 1933, convinced that this would be preferable to a return to fully functional democracy.

Weimar Germany had all the necessary components for democracy. However, the all-important balance between them was potentially flawed, in ways which could not have been apparent to the jurists who framed the Constitution and the politicians who amended it. Part of the pressure which distorted this balance came from internal malfunctions, and the rest from right-wing influences which exploited the imbalances and used the democratic constitution to destroy constitutional democracy.

Questions

1. Consider the arguments for and against the Weimar Republic being seen as an 'effective democracy'. Which is the stronger?
2. Article 48 of the Weimar Constitution has been called the 'suicide clause'. How apt is this description?

ANALYSIS (2): HOW RESPONSIBLE WERE THE POLITICAL PARTIES OF THE WEIMAR REPUBLIC?

The political parties of the Weimar Republic have been heavily criticised. Fraenkel, for example, maintains that they failed to fulfil 'the functions which devolve upon them in a constitutional pluralistic Parliamentary democracy'. (10) But this needs to be set in perspective. The range of parties and ideologies within Germany at this time was the widest ever experienced by any political system. Within the spectrum there were fairly consistent contrasts between those which supported the existence of the Republic and wished to maintain it, and those which opposed the Republic and tried to end it.

There was much that was positive about the contributions of the parties supporting the Republic. The four main groupings – the SPD, DDP, Z and DVP – all had roots in the Second Reich and had at one stage or another been involved in conflicts with Bismarck and his successors. The natural opposition within the Reich had therefore become the natural government within the Republic. Indeed, Bismarck had once predicted that the Centre and the SPD would come together if ever the Second Reich should collapse. (11)

Between them, the four parties played a crucial role in the formative years of the Republic. The SPD were the original keystone, providing both the first two Chancellors and the first President. The DDP played the major part in drafting the Constitution of 1919 and ensuring that it was based on the principles of liberal democracy. The DVP, although initially hostile, agreed to enter coalitions from 1923, and its leader, Stresemann, provided much needed stability up to 1929. The Centre was willing to serve in all coalitions and to maintain links between the SPD and parties of the right such as the DNVP. The moderate parties also ensured the survival of the Republic in the first 10 years of its existence. They eased its transition from a revolutionary regime into a permanent republic; they overcame the serious threats between 1920 and 1923; they presided over a more prosperous period from 1923 to 1929; and they provided a consensus within the Reichstag for developing a more positive foreign policy and relationship with France and Britain from 1925. Finally, they played a vital role in keeping democracy afloat in Prussia, Germany's largest state. Until 1932 this was administered by the SPD, with periodic support from the Centre. The administration proved more stable than that of the Republic as a whole and showed what political parties could do, even when confronted with the complexities of proportional representation and a fractured political spectrum.

So far we have a positive picture of moderation, responsibility and achievement, but the obvious fact is that the Republic did eventually collapse. Part of the reason must have been the failure of the moderate parties, despite their best intentions and efforts, to prevent it from doing so. There were unfortunately serious defects within each which, collectively, made possible the eventual triumph of anti-Republican forces.

Part of the responsibility for this must be taken by the SPD. Although by far the most important influence behind the formation of the Republic, it never quite managed to sustain a role in government proportionate to its size in the Reichstag. In the words of Hiden, 'They failed to make of their early association with the bourgeois parties, or so-called "democratic middle" of DDP, Centre and DVP, a lasting and constructive partnership.' (12) They refused, for example, to be involved in the government of the Republic during the crucial period between 1923 and 1928. During the period of the Weimar Republic the SPD remained essentially a party of the working class and made very little inroad into the middle classes. This was in contrast to the British Labour Party, which sought greater middle-class support as it became the main alternative to the Conservatives. Part of the problem for the SPD at this stage was that it was limited by attachments to its trade union movement and was concerned that any attempt at a more concerted appeal to the middle classes would lose it votes to the Communists.

The Centre Party was similarly limited by its sectional attachments, despite being the most consistent of all the parties in terms of electoral support. Its natural constituency was the Catholic vote, of which it always attracted over 50% (13). It had, however, little appeal to Protestants, despite professing to be primarily a 'Christian' party. But the most damaging impact of the Centre Party was its swing to the right. This occurred in two stages. In 1928 Monsignor Kaas took over from Wilhelm Marx as party leader, emphasising the party's clerical attachments and undermining its ability to reconcile the moderate parties on secular issues. Then after 1930 the Centre showed an unfortunate willingness to adapt to presidential dictatorship. Once Müller had withdrawn the SPD from government, Brüning was content to rely upon President Hindenburg to issue emergency decrees under Article 48 of the Constitution. Thus, after playing a key role in upholding democracy, the Centre delivered the first blows against it.

One of the great tragedies of the Weimar Republic was that the liberal democracy of the Constitution was not underpinned by a strong and cohesive liberal party. Indeed, Germany produced a unique political phenomenon: two liberal parties. To the left of centre, the DDP represented the political and social freedoms which made their way into Section II of the Constitution, while the DVP, on the right, merged liberal economic theory with nationalism and authority. The two parties rarely collaborated, apart from during the period of Stresemann's ascendancy, and neither was able to maintain the support of the middle classes, which should have been their natural constituency. In part, this was because they were never able to appeal to the 'diverse social and economic interests' which constituted the 'material base' of the middle classes. (14) The result was to be a devastating change in voting behaviour as, after 1928, the DDP and DVP lost almost all their electoral support to the Nazis. This defection was the greatest single factor in converting the latter from a fringe to a mass party. In a very real sense, therefore, fascism emerged from the ruins of liberalism.

Three parties meanwhile consistently defied the Republic and, according to Berghahn, 'promoted political ideas which could only be realised outside the existing constitutional framework'. (15) The Nazis initially tried to overthrow the Republic by revolution but, after the Munich Putsch, Hitler changed his strategy to one of long-term infiltration and subversion. He aimed after 1925 to achieve power legally, following which he would use the constitution to destroy the Weimar Republic. Revolution would therefore succeed rather than precede office. Despite the 'legal strategy', the Nazis intensified their propaganda offensive against the Republic and made full use of the opportunities offered to them by the Great Depression. As Broszat maintains, 'No other party – not even the KPD – was so dependent for its success on the crisis.' (16)

The DNVP was also subversive; despite brief periods of co-operation, its role was fundamentally destructive. Initially strongly against the Republic, it became more ambivalent during the 1920s. Some members served in the cabinet between 1924 and 1925. This was not through any reconciliation with the Republic, but rather to stake a claim to power and to keep out the SPD. Hugenberg, who took over the leadership of the DNVP in 1928, led it back to strong opposition to the institutions and policies of the Republic, collaborating increasingly with the Nazis. Hiden goes so far as to say that 'prominent members of the DNVP played handmaiden to Adolf Hitler and his movement at the close of the 1920s.' (17)

This was all part of a ghastly miscalculation on the part of the conservative right, which played directly into the hands of the far right. Attached to the DNVP were several constitutional theorists, who argued strongly for the further strengthening of the power of the presidency at the expense of the Reichstag, with the subsequent diminution of the role of party politics. The DNVP expected that the party system would fracture and that there would be a permanent broad front of the right. Hence the DNVP organ *Unsere Partei* proclaimed in 1931 that the party had transformed itself into 'a modern activist movement of the community as a whole'. (18) In September 1932 Hugenberg said that the DNVP would campaign 'not as a party but as the political army of the new state' and would serve 'the secret longing of those millions who to this day still find themselves entrapped in the slavery of the parties'. (19) These views were behind the DNVP's decision to co-operate closely with the NSDAP as an alternative to normal parliamentary-based party politics. But the DNVP completely miscalculated in their view that the Nazi Party would also dissolve into a national bund. Instead, the DNVP – and the nation – were to be absorbed into Nazism. All the DNVP succeeded in doing was to help Hitler replace a multi-party system by a one-party state.

The far left also had a role in the destruction of the Weimar Republic. They refused, in the crucial period after 1931, to collaborate with the moderate parties to save the Republic: there was, in other words, no coalition of the left and centre to hold back the advancing right. Why did this not happen? After all, the KPD had 89 seats after the July 1932 Reichstag election. Added to the 221 of the SPD, DDP, Centre and DVP, the combined total would have been 310, compared with the 247 of the DNVP and Nazis. But the KPD had strong reasons for not doing this. In addition to their bitter memories of 1919, they had an ideological perception of the future which could not include the Weimar Republic. Stalin instructed the KPD not to collaborate in any way with the rest of the left, regarding the SPD as 'social fascists', who gained 'the trust of the masses through fraud and treachery'. (20) In any case Thälmann, the leader of the KPD, saw Nazism as a catalyst for the eventual triumph of Communism. It would shake up bourgeois capitalism before collapsing in its turn – having cleared the way for a Communist revolution. According to this logic, it made no sense to help prolong the Republic. This would be particularly stupid since any movement of the KPD to the right could well lead to a defection of part of their vote to the SPD. The KPD were therefore indirectly, but knowingly, involved in the rise of Hitler by 1933.

Overall, three parties played a crucial part in ending the Republic. The roles of the DNVP and the NSDAP can be seen as destructive: they converted democracy into dictatorship. The KPD was obstructive: it took no action to save the Republic and it welcomed its going. Four parties tried to make the Republic work, but contained too many defects to succeed. The Centre Party was based too narrowly on sectional support. As such it was virtually a cross-section of the whole political spectrum and its internal right delivered the first blow to democracy. The DDP and DVP failed to underpin representative democracy with a liberal tradition which would appeal to the middle classes. The SPD failed to compromise at crucial moments in the Republic's history, when it might have provided the convergence of opposition to dictatorship.

Questions

1. Which of the moderate parties tried hardest to save the Republic?
2. Which delivered the greater blow to the Republic: the far right or the far left?

SOURCES

1. THE CONSTITUTION, REACTIONS AND DEVELOPMENTS

Source A: Extracts from the Constitution of the Weimar Republic (11 August 1919).

ARTICLE 1. The German Reich is a Republic. Political authority emanates from the people.

ARTICLE 5. Political authority is exercised in national affairs by the national government in accordance with the Constitution of the Reich, and in state affairs by the state governments in accordance with state constitutions.

ARTICLE 17. Every state must have a republican constitution. The representatives of the people must be elected by universal, equal, direct, and secret suffrage of all German citizens, both men and women, in accordance with the principles of proportional representation.

ARTICLE 22. The delegates [of the Reichstag] are elected by universal, equal, direct, and secret suffrage by men and women over twenty years of age, according to the principle of proportional representation. Election day must be a Sunday or a public holiday.

ARTICLE 23. The Reichstag is elected for four years. New elections must take place at the latest on the sixtieth day after this term has run its course.

ARTICLE 41. The Reich President is elected by the whole German people. Every German who has completed his thirty-fifth year is eligible for election.

ARTICLE 43. The term of office of the Reich President is seven years. Re-election is possible.

ARTICLE 48. If any state does not fulfil the duties imposed upon it by the Constitution or the laws of the Reich, the Reich President may enforce such duties with the aid of the armed forces.

In the event that the public order and security are seriously disturbed or endangered, the Reich President may take the measures necessary for their restoration, intervening, if necessary, with the aid of the armed forces. For this purpose he may abrogate temporarily, wholly or in part, the fundamental principles laid down in Articles 114, 115, 117, 116, 123, 124 and 153.

ARTICLE 52. The Reich Cabinet consists of the Reich Chancellor and the Reich Ministers.

ARTICLE 53. The Reich Chancellor and, on his recommendation, the Reich Ministers, are appointed and dismissed by the Reich President.

ARTICLE 54. The Reich Chancellor and the Reich Ministers require for the exercise of their office the confidence of the Reichstag. Any one of them must resign if the Reichstag by formal resolution withdraws its confidence.

ARTICLE 60. A Reichsrat is formed to give the German states representation in the law-making and administration of the Reich.

ARTICLE 61. Each state has at least one vote in the Reichsrat. In the case of the larger states one vote shall be assigned for every million inhabitants ... No single state shall have more than two-fifths of the total number of votes.

ARTICLE 63. The states shall be represented in the Reichsrat by members of their governments.

ARTICLE 109. All Germans are equal before the law. Men and women have the same fundamental civil rights and duties. Public legal privileges or disadvantages of birth or of rank are abolished. Titles of nobility may be bestowed no longer.

ARTICLE 114. Personal liberty is inviolable.

ARTICLE 118. Every German has the right, within the limits of the general laws, to express his opinion freely ... Censorship is forbidden.

ARTICLE 124. All Germans have the right to form associations and societies for purposes not contrary to the criminal law.

ARTICLE 135. All inhabitants of the Reich enjoy full religious freedom and conscience.

ARTICLE 136. There is no state church.

ARTICLE 144. The entire school system is under the control of the state.

ARTICLE 153. The right of private property is guaranteed by the Constitution.

ARTICLE 159. Freedom of association for the preservation and promotion of labour and economic conditions is guaranteed to everyone and to all vocations.

Source B: from an article *The German Democracy* by Ernst Troeltsch (29 December 1918).

Overnight we have become the most radical democracy in Europe.

Source C: Extract from *Politics as a Vocation*, a lecture given by Max Weber in Munich in 1920.

It is not summer's bloom that lies before us, but first of all a polar night of icy darkness and severity, whichever group may be outwardly victorious at present. For where there is nothing, it is not only the Kaiser but the proletarian too who has lost his rights. When this night slowly begins to fade, who of those will be left still living whose spring has now, to all appearances, been clad in such luxuriant blossom? And what will by then have become the inner lives of you all?

Source D: Carl von Ossietzky's criticism of the Republic, September 1924.

Our republic is not yet an object of mass consciousness but a constitutional document and a governmental administration ... Around this state, lacking any ideas and with an eternally guilty conscience, there are grouped a couple of so-called constitutional parties, likewise lacking an idea and with no better conscience, which are not led but administered. Administered by a bureaucratic caste that is responsible for the misery of recent years in domestic and foreign affairs and that smothers all signs of fresh life with a cold hand.

Source E: the number of sittings of the Reichstag.

Year	Sessions
1930	94
1931	41
1932	13

Source F: the number of decrees issued under Article 48 of the Constitution.

Year	Decrees
1930	5
1931	44
1932	60

QUESTIONS

*1. Explain the references to 'proportional representation' (Source A) and 'Kaiser' (Source C). [2]
2. What do the tone and language of Sources C and D have in common and in what ways do they differ? [5]
3. To what extent do Sources E and F prove that there was a drift towards dictatorship in the last years of the Weimar Republic? [4]
4. How reliable are Sources E and F to the historian studying democracy within the Weimar Republic? What other types of source might be used to supplement them? [6]

5. Using Sources A to F, and your own knowledge, to what extent does Source A support the view expressed in Source B? [8]

Worked answer

*1. [This question requires a short but precise answer. You should bear in mind that only two marks are allocated.]

'Proportional representation' relates the number of seats to each party in the legislature to the proportion of total votes cast. The Kaiser was the former Emperor of the Second Reich, who abdicated in November 1919.

SOURCES

2. POLITICAL PARTIES, ELECTIONS AND PROGRAMMES

Source G: A ballot form for the 1930 Reichstag election: district of Schleswig-Holstein (The main parties on this form are: 1. Social Democrats (SPD); 2. National Party (DNVP); 3. Centre (Z); 4. Communists (KPD); 5. People's Party (DVP); 9. Nazis (NSDAP).

[See Figure 1, p. 29.]

Source H: Reichstag election results 1919–33.

[See Figure 2, p. 30.]

Source I: extracts from the Programme of the Centre Party (Z): 1922.

As a Christian party of the people: the national community of Germans; the realization of Christian principles in the state, society, economy and culture . . . Rejection of violent overthrow, repudiation of the all-powerful state.
    . . . Commitment to the German national state; self-government; the professional civil service as the backbone of government. The dominance of a class or caste is incompatible with the essence of the national state.
    . . . Solidarity of all social strata and professions; rejection of class struggle and class domination.
    . . . Safeguarding of freedom of conscience, religious freedom, and the freedom of education . . . The freedom and independence of ecclesiastical communities and

Reichstagswahl
Wahlkreis Schleswig-Holstein

1	Sozialdemokratische Partei Deutschlands Schroeder, Daske — Eggerstedt — Jühler — Diefer	1	○
2	Deutschnationale Volkspartei Oberfohren — Gerns — Wölfing von Ditten — Goth	2	○
3	Zentrum Brüning — Käfers — Juchs, Dedwig — Germershausen	3	○
4	Kommunistische Partei Thälmann — Augustat, Gille — Drud — Jühri	4	○
5	Deutsche Volkspartei Dr. Schiffers — Fischer — Cimbal, Cilsabeth — Drhns	5	○
5a	Christlich-soziale Volksgemeinschaft Drederies — Grojinger — Wagner	5a	○
6	Deutsche Staatspartei Daußen — Dr. Ridz-Wiemich, Cmilie — Ubjelb Chlregge	6	○
7	Reichspartei des Deutschen Mittelstandes (Wirtschaftspartei) Köhler — Kremers — Museleibt — Köhler	7	○
9	Nationalsozialistische Deutsche Arbeiterpartei (Hitlerbewegung) Dronjen — Meyer-Quade — Thormöhlen — Gtomer	9	○
10	Bauern- u. Landvolkpartei Schleswig-Holstein (Christlich-Nationale Bauern- und Landvolkpartei) Schleis — Köhler — Mangelfen — Bohrnd	10	○
11a	Volksrechtpartei (Reichspartei für Volksrecht und Aufwertung) und Christlich-Soziale Reichspartei Graf Dolabotostz-Wehnen—Jlef—Dennigen—Rulzheri	11a	○
11b	Volksrechtpartei Merls — Mohr — Köhler — Kverdel .	11b	○
12	Deutsche Bauernpartei Cra — Wulff — Herrenberg — Gäfer	12	○
16	Treviranus-Konservative Volkspartei Zirbranus — Cambach — Kleger — von Ubfeleb	16	○
17	Christlich-sozialer Volksdienst Matthiefen — Theefen — Bautfen — Gtolze	17	○
19a	Polnische Volkspartei Lebtwolat — Lalonkyd — Sybot — Kwirinkiroll	19a	○
19b	Schleswigscher Verein Sögaard — Detersen — Jhort — Lassen	19b	○
19c	Friesland Oldfen — Hemkingfen — Detersen — Lorenzen	19c	○
23	Unabhängige Sozialdemokratische Partei Deutschlands Lirbnecht — Wiegmann, Gille — Heiber — Schröder	23	○
24	Haus- und Grundbesitzer Wehnert — Kohlmorgen — Krobed — Schramm	24	○
28	Menschheitspartei und Neue Volksgemeinschaft Schober — Krampel — Thiel — Duus	28	○

Figure 1 A ballot form for the 1930 Reichstag election: district of Schleswig-Holstein

Source: G. Soldan, ed.: *Zeitgeschichte in Wort und Bild* (Oldenburg 1934), III, 333, reproduced in J. Remark, ed.: *The Nazi Years* (Englewood Cliffs, NJ 1969), 22.

Party	Jan 1919	June 1920	May 1924	Dec 1924	May 1928	Sept 1930	July 1932	Nov 1932	Mar 1933
NSDAP	–	–	6.6 (32)	3.0 (14)	2.6 (12)	18.3 (107)	37.3 (230)	33.1 (196)	43.9 (288)
DNVP Nationalists	10.3 (44)	14.9 (71)	19.5 (95)	20.5 (103)	14.2 (73)	7.0 (41)	5.9 (37)	8.3 (52)	8.0 (52)
DVP	4.4 (19)	13.9 (65)	9.2 (45)	10.1 (51)	8.7 (45)	4.5 (30)	1.2 (7)	1.9 (11)	1.1 (2)
DDP Democrats	18.6 (75)	8.3 (39)	5.7 (28)	6.3 (32)	4.9 (25)	3.8 (20)	1.0 (4)	1.0 (2)	0.9 (5)
Z Centre	(91)	13.6 (64)	13.4 (65)	13.6 (69)	12.1 (62)	11.8 (68)	12.5 (75)	11.9 (70)	(74)
	(19.7)								(11.2)
BVP Bavarian People's Party		4.3 (21)	2.2 (16)	3.7 (19)	3.0 (16)	3.0 (19)	3.4 (22)	3.1 (20)	(10)
SPD Socialists	37.9 (165)	21.6 (102)	20.5 (100)	26.0 (131)	29.8 (153)	24.5 (143)	21.6 (133)	20.4 (121)	18.3 (120)
USPD Independent Socialists	7.6 (22)	17.9 (8.1)	0.8	–	–	–	–	–	–
KPD Communists	–	2.1 (4)	12.6 (62)	9.0 (45)	10.6 (54)	13.1 (77)	14.3 (89)	16.9 (100)	12.3 (8.1)
Others*	1.5	3.4	9.8	7.8	14.1	13.9	2.8	3.4	4.3
Percentage of electorate voting	82.7	78.4	76.3	77.7	74.6	81.4	83.4	79.9	88.0

Figure 2   Reichstag election results 1919–33

Source: R. Wolfson: *Years of Change* (London 1978), 289.

the safeguarding of their influence on the life of the people. The cooperation of state and church without violation of their mutual independence.

Source J: extracts from the Programme of the Social Democratic Party (SPD): 1925.

The democratic republic offers the most favourable ground for the liberation of the working class and therefore for the development of socialism.

. . . Protection against all monarchical and militarist strivings. Transformation of the armed forces of the Reich into a reliable organ of the republic.

. . . The defence of workers, white-collar employees, and civil-service employees and the elevation of living standards for the broad masses demands: Defence of the freedom of association and the right to strike . . . Equal rights for women in the workplace . . . Comprehensive, preventing, enlightening, and effective measures in the area of popular welfare, in particular as regards education, health and economic concerns.

. . . The public institutions of education, schooling, culture, and research are secular. All legally grounded interference in these institutions by churches and religious or ideological communities is to be opposed. Separation of church and state. Separation of church and schools . . . No expenditure of public monies for ecclesiastical or religious purposes.

. . . In the struggle against the capitalist system, the Social Democratic Party demands: Land, property, mineral resources, and natural sources of energy supplies are to be withdrawn from the system of capitalist exploitation and transferred to the service of the whole community.

. . . As a member of the Socialist Workers' International, the Social Democratic Party of Germany struggles together with the workers of all nations against imperialist and fascist advances and for the realization of socialism.

. . . It demands the peaceful resolution of international conflicts.

. . . It demands international disarmament.

Source K: extracts from the Programme of the German People's Party (DVP), 1931.

Fatherland. All of our thoughts, our burning desires, and our struggles are dedicated to the greatness and freedom of the fatherland. A people, whose Lebensraum has been brutally cut down, whose freedom to live has been cast into chains through senseless treaties . . . can only wrestle its way back up through the strength of its love for the fatherland and national solidarity. Over many years Marxism has been breeding a sickly international and pacifist romanticism in the place of a resolute will devoted to the fatherland.

Freedom. Our faith and our view of life is rooted in the spiritual soil created in the times of Bismarck and Bennigsen and before them the great minds of German idealism . . . The freedom that we mean is that of the morally responsible individual. All moral responsibility, however, is rooted in faith and religiosity. Revolution and socialism have bred a desolate materialism, the struggle of classes against one another.

State. We are fighting against the caricature of a dictatorial state that enslaves the free life of national forces.

Constitution. Everything in constitutional life that is un-German and alien to our nature, everything that places the rule of the masses in the place of the rule of achievement, must be overcome . . . We are opposed to the exaggeration of parliamentarianism.

Questions

1. Explain the references to 'Reich' (Source J) and 'Bismarck' (Source K). [2]
2. To what extent do Sources G and H show the advantages and disadvantages of proportional representation in the Weimar Republic? [5]
3. What are the advantages and disadvantages of Sources I, J and K to the historian studying party politics in the Weimar Republic? [6]
4. 'The Centre Party and the SPD differed entirely in their views of the relationship between church and state.' Do Sources I and J prove this? [5]
*5. 'The Centre Party, SPD and DVP were naturally antagonistic and therefore likely to be bad partners in any coalition government.' Using Sources I, J and K and your own knowledge, do you consider this view to be correct? [7]

Worked answer

*5. [This question would probably have the longest response on most examination papers. It requires comparisons and contrasts between selected examples from all three sources. It also needs a degree of additional knowledge to show the limitations of the documents as sources.]

Sources I, J and K certainly reveal fundamental differences between the three parties. For example, the Centre Party's 'rejection of class struggle and class domination' (Source I) is clearly aimed at the SPD's ambitions for 'the realization of socialism' (Source J). Similarly, the Centre's commitment to safeguarding ecclesiastical influence 'on the life of the people' (Source I) seems directly contrary to the SPD's opposition to 'all legally grounded interference' by the churches. The programme of the DVP strongly attacks the SPD, even if by thinly veiled implication, through references to 'a sickly international and pacifist romanticism' and 'a desolate materialism' (Source K).

On the other hand, the sources also indicate areas of common interest and concern. The Centre's belief in 'solidarity of all social strata and professions' is not essentially different to the SPD's 'defence of workers, white-collar employees, and civil-service employees', while the Centre's aim for 'cooperation' between state and church 'without violation of their mutual independence' is not necessarily incompatible with the SPD's 'separation of church and state'. It is true that the DVP programme appears more nationalistic than either of its counterparts but even here there are phrases, such as 'the morally responsible individual', which would have been approved by the SPD and Centre; the latter would certainly have accepted that moral responsibility should be 'rooted in faith and religiosity' (Source K).

The three sources provide a limited overall perspective. This is partly due to their nature as sources; party programmes are bound to be polemical and it is easy to find conflicting catchphrases. But the 1920s also saw a considerable degree of co-operation in day-to-day politics. The parties found it possible to co-exist in coalition with each other. Chancellors emerged from all three, including Marx (1923–25) from the Centre and Muller (1928–30) from the SPD, while Stresemann (Chancellor in 1923 and then Foreign Minister) had a considerable personal influence on the development of consensus politics between 1923 and 1929. At least until the financial crisis of 1929 their pragmatic approach softened the apparent antagonisms between their party programmes.

3

VERSAILLES
AND ITS IMPACT

BACKGROUND NARRATIVE

Germany signed on armistice with the Allies on 11 November 1918. From this point onwards, negotiations for a peace settlement were carried out between the Allies in Paris, within the format of the Council of Ten. Most of the work was done by President Wilson of the United States, Lloyd George, the British Prime Minister, and Clemenceau, the French Premier. A preliminary draft of the arrangements concerning Germany was sent to the German government, but any attempts made by the new Republic to change the terms were rejected.

The Treaty of Versailles was signed on 28 June 1919. It affirmed, by Article 231, the responsibility of Germany and her Allies for the outbreak of the First World War and accordingly made provision for territorial adjustments, demilitarisation and economic compensation to the victorious Allies for the losses they had incurred. Germany was deprived of Alsace-Lorraine, Eupen and Malmédy, Northern Schleswig, Posen, West Prussia, parts of southern Silesia, and all her overseas colonies. Limits were placed upon her naval capacity, her army was restricted to 100,000 volunteers, and the Rhineland was demilitarised. A considerable quantity of rolling-stock and merchant shipping was also removed, while France was given exclusive rights to the coal-mines in the Saar region. Finally, provision was made for the payment of reparations by the German government, the total amount eventually being fixed in 1921 at 136,000 million gold marks.

The terms caused considerable resentment within Germany and contributed to the spiralling inflation which undermined the economy between 1921 and 1923. Attempts were made to regularise the payment of reparations by the Dawes Plan (1924) and the Young Plan (1929); the result was to spread the load, extend the deadlines and provide American investments. Following the impact of the Great Depression, most of the reparations were finally cancelled at Lausanne in 1932. The military and territorial terms of the Treaty were undermined by the unilateral action taken by Hitler after 1933.

Whether this was an unwise settlement depends upon the precise wording of the question asked. The first analysis puts forward the view that, in objective terms, the case against the Treaty has been overstated. The second, however, points to the Treaty acting as a catalyst for negative influences within the Weimar Republic itself.

ANALYSIS (1): WAS THE TREATY OF VERSAILLES A 'CARTHAGINIAN' PEACE?

At the height of the Punic Wars, a Roman senator demanded the complete destruction of Carthage: 'delenda est Carthago.' The term 'Carthaginian peace' has remained synonymous with the severe and vindictive treatment of a conquered enemy.

The traditional view of the Treaty of Versailles is that it inflicted harsh and unjust terms upon Germany. Foremost among its contemporary critics were J.M. Keynes and Harold Nicolson, who expressed disgust with the way in which the terms were drawn up. Some historians adopted a similar view. W.H. Dawson, for example, emphasised that the Treaty cut into German territory in a way which blatantly discriminated in favour of non-German populations. This approach has, however, been extensively modified, partly by comparison with the settlement after the Second World War and partly as a result of new perspectives created by revisionist historians such as Bariéty, McDougall, Schuker and Trachtenberg. (1) It is therefore possible to put an altogether more positive interpretation on the Treaty of Versailles. We should start by not being too dismissive of the statesmen who drew up the settlement. It is true that they were accountable to their populations and that they therefore had to pursue the national interest. But this does not preclude a logical and pragmatic analysis of international needs reinforced by purely national concerns; this is evident in the settlement as a whole and especially within the French position. There had to be three main priorities: to guarantee Europe against the possibility of future German aggression; to revive the economic infrastructure of the Allies; and to ensure the stability of the new nation states in central and eastern Europe. None of these was inherently revanchist.

The military provisions of the Treaty may appear harsh. The army was limited to 100,000 volunteers and the navy to 6 battleships; the air force was abolished and the Rhineland was demilitarised. Yet these measures need to be seen within the context of the military power of Germany. The combined forces of Britain, the Empire, France, Russia and Italy had been insufficient to defeat the Second Reich and it needed the intervention of the United States to guarantee Allied victory. It therefore made sense to limit the base for any future military recovery by such a formidable opponent. In any case, the argument that the war had been engineered by Germany, explicitly stated in Article 231, was not entirely propaganda. A substantial number of historians, mainly German, have now demonstrated that the foreign policy of the Second Reich aimed at a war sooner rather than later as a means of breaking the Franco-Russian alliance and achieving an early form of Lebensraum in eastern Europe. This line has been taken especially by Fischer, Berghahn and Röhl. In this light, the military provisions were not excessively harsh. There was only a limited Allied occupation and there was no zoning, as was to occur in 1945. Germany was also allowed some means of self-defence. The provision for 100,000 volunteers was actually in Germany's favour, since it allowed for the development of a professional core upon which subsequent military recovery could be constructed. Finally, it seems that the Allies could have gone much further. They drew up plans to invade the Reich should the terms of the Treaty be refused. Yet they did not do so, even though Hindenburg and Groener made it clear to the German government that ultimately nothing could stop them. This shows a degree of restraint and moderation on the part of the Allies not entirely born of war-weariness.

The transfer of territory to France, Belgium and Denmark was also limited in scope. The return of Alsace-Lorraine to France, after its conquest by Prussia in 1871, was inevitable. Giving the small industrial regions of Eupen and Malmédy to Belgium was intended to reconstruct the latter's industrial infrastructure, while the incorporation of northern Schleswig into Denmark after plebiscite simply reversed the annexation of the area by Bismarck in 1864. The transfer of resources was more controversial, inviting criticism from J.M. Keynes that the iron and coal provisions were 'inexpedient and disastrous'. German opinion was also incensed by Article 231, the 'War Guilt Clause' which was used to justify reparations. Yet the purpose of this was overstated. Heiber maintains: 'The very fact that this paragraph was not embodied in the preamble or immediately following it, but was given such an astronomical serial number and almost hidden in the undergrowth of the treaty, suggests that it originally had no programmatic significance.' (2) French revanchism was not, as has so often been suggested, the key factor in the financial provisions; there is a strong argument that they were needed to rebuid the shattered infrastructure of both France and Belgium, whose territory – not Germany's – had borne the destruction of four years of warfare. Germany's industries, by contrast, had remained untouched. Trachtenberg argues that the French were far more moderate in their expectations from reparations than were the British, while Bariéty maintains that they were seeking not to dismantle or cripple Germany but to establish a Franco-German equilibrium on the Continent: part of the process had to be a greater economic balance between the two powers.

The establishment of new nation states in central and eastern Europe has invited the criticism that Germany became the victim of the unfair use of the principle of national self-determination. There is something in this, as over six million Germans found themselves outside the Reich. On the other hand, the Allies, in the words of King Leopold of the Belgians, 'did what they could'. The new states were not entirely the product of Wilsonian idealism. They were already a *fait accompli*, emerging from the collapse of the Austro-Hungarian and Russian Empires in 1918. They needed in 1919 to be given a chance of survival, not only against Germany but also against Soviet Russia, which Mayer sees as the main threat to Europe. (3) The logic of their security was that in certain cases national self-determination had to be applied against Germany. There are two examples of this. Poland, brought into existence by the Treaty of Brest-Litovsk – which Germany had imposed upon a defeated Russia – needed access to the sea to be economically viable. This meant the use of the port of Danzig which, as a concession to the German population, was placed under the control of the League of Nations. Posen and West Prussia were essential as the hinterland to the Baltic, and in any case had a majority of Poles within the population. The other example was the settlement in central Europe, which confirmed Czechoslovakia in possession of the German-speaking Sudetenland and prevented the possibilty of an Anschluss, or union, between Germany and German-speaking Austria. In both cases there could have been no sensible alternative. Neither area had previously belonged to Germany and incorporating the Sudenland into Austria would have made geographical nonsense. In any case, it was necessary for Czechoslovakia's industrial viability. As for meeting popular demands for an Anschluss, this would have created a Germany far stronger than that of 1914. How would this have established a balance in western Europe or provided protection for the newly independent states of central and eastern Europe?

In all of these cases, therefore, the intention was to constrain, not to crush, Germany. The framework of the settlement was bound to have flaws but it was intended that these should be reviewed within the context of the League of Nations, the Covenant of which was incorporated into the Treaty of Versailles. Unfortunately there were two major difficulties, which undermined any possibility of revision and thereby prevented early reconciliation between Germany and the Allies.

The first was the decision at the outset not to involve Germany in any of the discussions leading to the Treaty. This was undoubtedly a serious mistake since the German government had no part-ownership of the settlement and was bound to react to it as a diktat conceived in the spirit of hostility rather than of compromise. The implications of this are examined in Analysis (2), below. But the motive behind this exclusion was not vindictiveness: rather, it was an attempt to draw a lesson from history. This is always dangerous for polticians since the real lesson of history is that precedents, like lessons, are multi-faceted. Parallels were made with the Second Congress of Vienna (1815), at which Talleyrand, representative of defeated France, had managed to drive a diplomatic wedge between victorious Britain, Russia, Austria and Prussia. As it turned out, Wilson, Clemenceau and Lloyd George managed to fall out quite effectively without German help and Brockdorff-Rantzau, a mere privy councillor who was summoned to receive the terms, had none of the more positive aims of Talleyrand to sell the settlement to his government. Germany was therefore never able to live with Versailles as France had with Vienna.

The second obstacle to reconciliation was the failure of the settlement's intended safety-valve, the League of Nations. This was due to an entirely unforeseen factor: the withdrawal of the United States following the failure of Congress in 1920 to ratify President Wilson's signature. As a result, the League struggled to find a meaningful role, and future reconciliation with Germany had to be attempted not through the League but through agreements, like the Locarno Pact (1925) which paid lip-service to the League. The moderating influence of the United States was also badly missed after 1920. It might eventually have reconciled the Weimar Republic with the more positive principles of Versailles and it would certainly have given France the sense of security which she increasingly missed. American involvement could therefore have done much to reduce the underlying antipathy between Germany and France.

Objectively, the terms of the Treaty of Versailles can largely be justified by the need to safeguard against the very real threat posed by Germany, to rebuild France and Belgium and to give viability to the new democracies of Europe. But the process was complicated by the failure of the Allies to involve the German government at any stage in the Treaty's formulation, and of the League of Nations to carry out its intended moderating role in its fulfilment. Thus, like Carthage, Germany came to see itself as a victim without actually being destroyed.

Questions

1. 'The real problem with the Treaty of Versailles was not the terms themselves but the refusal to allow Germany any part in drawing them up.' Do you agree?
2. 'Germany could expect little else apart from the Versailles Settlement.' Do you agree?

ANALYSIS (2): WAS THE TREATY OF VERSAILLES A DISASTER FOR THE WEIMAR REPUBLIC?

It has been argued that the Republic was brought down primarily because of the deep opposition to it engendered by the Treaty of Versailles which made possible the rise of Hitler. Zimmerman maintained in 1968 that 'Timely revision of the peace treaties would have saved the Weimar Republic and saved the peace.' (4) The pendulum now seems to have swung the other way. Hillgruber argues that the time when the Republic was most vulnerable to the Treaty of Versailles (1919–23) was precisely the time that it survived, whereas the Treaty's importance was 'relatively small by the end of the Stresemann era'. (5) It could certainly be argued that by the time Hitler came to power in 1933 the reparations issue had been resolved by the Lausanne settlement and that, in any case, foreign policy and Versailles were no longer the most important issues in the collapse of the Weimar Republic.

But this has gone too far in the other direction. The impact of Versailles was important in undermining German democracy – not because it acted directly in the rise of Hitler but because it produced several key influences which continued to grow long after the Treaty itself had ceased to be critical. In this way, the Treaty was itself a catalyst for, rather than a direct cause of, the collapse of the Republic. This operated in four ways.

In the first place, Versailles created a deep and widespread resentment throughout the entire population. Germans had already suffered severely during the closing stages of the war as a direct result of the British blockade and they assumed that Germany would have a genuine share of any post-war settlement. Hence, although they expected to lose Alsace-Lorraine to France, possibly West Prussia to Poland, and even some overseas colonies, they hoped to gain Austria and the Sudetenland from the now defunct Austro-Hungarian Empire. The actual terms therefore came as a profound blow. Wilson's principle of national self-determination seemed to operate against Germans everywhere and in favour of Germans nowhere. Even more resented, however, was Article 231 of the Treaty – the War Guilt Clause – which provided the justification for the fixing of reparations. The peace delegation under Brockdorff-Rantzau protested vigorously against this and other terms but was utterly helpless in the face of Allied intransigence.

Such resentment was increasingly targeted against the Republic for having signed what the media unanimously labelled a 'disgraceful' document. This was actually unjust. Scheidemann's administration had done everything possible to get the terms revised and had even questioned Hindenburg about the possibility of military resistance; but, in the end, to save Germany from an Allied invasion, the Treaty had to be accepted by Bauer's government. The danger was that people of moderate views would ignore the circumstances and attribute blame, thus seeing the Republic as tainted at the outset. The government, quite unintentionally, contributed to this threat. Stung by the perceived injustice of the War Guilt Clause, the Foreign Ministry employed historians to prove that Germany was not responsible for the outbreak of the war, and that the destruction was therefore a responsibility shared by all the participants. But the side-effect was to rehabilitate the reputation of the German army, releasing it from any association with aggression and militarism.

This, in turn, revived the cause of the conservative right, which had a strong attachment to the memory of the Second Reich and instinctively distrusted the Weimar Republic. The new regime had provided military conservatism with the sort of logic it needed. If the German army had not been instrumental in starting the First World War then it followed that its defeat was a matter for profound regret. Taken a stage further, this defeat could be seen as an act of political betrayal by the Republican government. By trying to connect the situation before 1919 with the iniquities of Versailles in order to disprove German war guilt, the Republic unintentionally gave the conservative right the opportunity to foster the legend of the 'stab in the back'. This phrase was actually introduced by Hindenburg in November 1919 before a parliamentary committee of the National Assembly. During his campaign for the Presidency in 1925 Hindenburg sought to justify his and Ludendorff's abdication of military responsibility in October 1918 by rewriting history in just this way. The result is seen by most historians as a serious liability for the Republic: Heiber goes so far as to say that the 'war guilt lie' became 'a dangerous explosive charge'.

This is especially apt when considering the offensive launched against the Republic by the Nazis at the end of the 1920s and the beginning of the 1930s. Hitler's strange amalgam of fringe ideas was given greater credibility and popular appeal by his emphasis on two mainstream policies. One was his widespread use of the 'stab in the back' and the 'Versailles diktat'. These enabled the NSDAP to collaborate closely with conservative forces within the DNVP, the army and business, which enhanced Hitler's reputation at a crucial stage in his party's development. He also projected the NSDAP as the party which would offer economic salvation to the middle classes suffering under the impact of the depression after 1929 and, as a result, enormously increased the NSDAP's electoral support in the elections of 1930 and 1932.

The economic situation which made this possible again had a connection with Versailles, although the nature of this connection needs to be precisely identified. Complications over the reparations bill set in accordance with the Treaty of Versailles subsequently led to the establishment of a financial network which eventually collapsed after 1929. It was this system, not the reparations themselves, which proved disastrous for the German economy.

The initial liability was considerable: in April 1921 the Allied Reparations Commission set the reparations bill at 132,000 million gold marks. Tied to this was a condition that 12,000 million would be paid in advance, followed by 2000 million per annum and 26% of the value of Germany's exports. It would be an exaggeration to say that this was the sole cause of the great inflation between 1921 and 1923, but having to ship out substantial capital sums (50% to France, 22%

to Britain, 10% to Italy and 8% to Belgium) must have been a major factor in the collapse of the mark. It is true that the government could have limited the extent of the inflation by increasing levels of domestic taxation rather than printing notes, but it very much wanted to avoid this course, which would only further antagonise a population already infuriated by the burden of 'war guilt'. In any case, economic crisis would oblige the Allies to confront reality: that their demands were just too harsh.

The attempt to rationalise reparations led to a new economic order, the Dawes Plan of 1924 setting up a new chain of dependency. By this means, Germany provided reparations payments to Britain, France and Italy who, in turn, were enabled to pay off their war debts to the United States. These returned as loans to Germany. The alternative would have been for Britain and France to have reduced their dependence on German reparations in return for cancellation of the war debts; the United States, however, insisted that these should be paid in full. The famous triangular pattern was therefore firmly set.

Great damage was to be inflicted on the German economy, not by the continued payment of reparations, but rather by the loans upon which Germany depended in order to sustain an economy capable of paying reparations. At first the role of American investment was highly beneficial. In the period immediately after 1924, Germany received some 16,000 million marks compared with the 7,000 million she actually paid out. This helped to replenish the home market which had been stripped of assets as a result of the inflation. Industrial production expanded, full employment was achieved and there were even salary increases in the public sector. But the problem was that this expansion was highly vulnerable. It did not affect the large-scale consumer industries at home, such as motor vehicles, and it did not have the full infrastructure of export sales. The cycle of dependence therefore remained – and this was dramatically disrupted by the Wall Street Crash in October 1929. From that time onwards the German economy spiralled into depression, resulting in decreased production, foreclosures and 6 million unemployed. The speed with which this happened was linked to the terms of the American loans: they were all short term and subject to repayment on demand. Hence it made little difference that reparations had been extensively rescheduled by the Young Plan in 1929 or virtually cancelled at Lausanne in 1932. Economic catastrophe still occurred, although it was brought about by the loans which reparations had engendered, not by the reparations themselves.

In summary, the terms of the Treaty came as a shock to the people, who blamed the government of the Republic. This condemnation remained with the Republic as a result of the 'stab in the back' myth, which brought collaboration between the conservative right and the radical right. The Republic became particularly vulnerable with the collapse of the economy after 1929. This owed much to the establishment of a new network of dependency to replace the initial problems created by the reparations payments. The Treaty of Versailles therefore set in motion influences which were to prove more damaging to the Republic than the Treaty itself. Its impact was therefore indirect, but real nevertheless.

Questions

1. What is the connection between the 'stab in the back' myth and the Treaty of Versailles?
2. Which was more important in undermining the Weimar Republic: the 'stab in the back' myth or the reparations payments?

SOURCES

1. WAR GUILT

Source A: an extract from the Treaty of Versailles, 28 June 1919.

PART VIII
Article 231. The Allied and Associated Governments affirm and Germany accepts the responsibility of Germany and her allies for causing all the loss and damage to which the Allied and Associated Governments have been subjected as a consequence of the war imposed upon them by the aggression of Germany and her allies.

Source B: from a speech by Count Ulrich von Brockdorff-Rantzau to the German Delegation, Versailles, 7 May 1919.

The demand is made that we shall acknowledge that we alone are guilty of having caused the war. Such a confession in my mouth would be a lie. We are far from seeking to escape from any responsibility for this world war and for its having been waged as it has. The attitude of the former German government . . . and its omissions in the tragic twelve days in July may have contributed to the catastrophe, but we emphatically deny that the people of Germany, who were convinced that they were waging a war of defence, should be burdened with the sole guilt of that war.

Source C: from the Report presented to the Preliminary Peace Conference, 1919.

CONCLUSIONS

1. The war was premeditated by the Central Powers together with their Allies, Turkey and Bulgaria, and was the result of acts committed in order to make it unavoidable.
2. Germany, in agreement with Austria-Hungary, deliberately worked to defeat all the many conciliatory proposals made by the Entente Powers and their repeated efforts to avoid war.

Source D: from *The Case for the Central Powers*, 1925.

SEVENTEEN CONCLUSIONS

1. Germany pursued no aim either in Europe or elsewhere which could only be achieved by means of war. Austria's only aim was to maintain the status quo.
2. Germany's preparations for war were on a considerably smaller scale than those made by France . . . As compared with Russia's armaments, those of Austria-Hungary were absolutely inadequate. . . .
13. Russia was the first Power to order general mobilization. France was the first Power to inform another Power officially of her decision to take part in a European war.
14. England was never as firm in advising moderation in St Petersburg as Germany in giving this advice to Vienna.
15. Germany's premature declaration of war on Russia was a political error, which can be accounted for by the immense danger of the position on two fronts . . . The decisive event was not this or that declaration of war, but the action which made the declaration of war inevitable, and this action was Russia's general mobilization.
16. England declared war on Germany because she did not consider it compatible with her interests that France should be defeated a second time. . . .

Questions

1. Apart from Austria-Hungary, who were the two 'allies' of Germany in the First World War (Source A)? [2]
    Which state declined to enter on Germany's side? [1]
*2. Do Sources A to D show that establishing war guilt was the primary purpose of the Treaty of Versailles and the main focus of opposition to it? [6]
3. How effectively do the arguments in Source D refute those in Source C? What other types of source would help to answer this question? [6]
4. 'There was an overwhelming argument for Germany having started the First World War.' Do these sources, and your own knowledge, support this view? [10]

Worked answer

*2. [The answer to this question is to be found largely within the sources themselves, although a sense of background perspective needs to be made evident to clarify the overall argument. Some additional material may therefore be useful.]

A more effective inference from Sources A to D would be that war guilt was not intended by the Allies to be the most apparent part of the Treaty of Versailles but that it became the part to which Germans most strongly objected.

References to war guilt could have been mentioned in the preamble or in Part I or even in Article 1. Instead, they did not appear until Part VIII, Article 231. They were not, therefore, the primary purpose of the Treaty. Nevertheless, war guilt was intended to be the legal basis for the reparations provisions in the rest of Part VIII by establishing 'the responsibility of Germany and her Allies' for the losses (Source A). For this reason, the Allies were careful to provide historical 'evidence' (Source C) for the war being 'premeditated by the Central Powers', who had 'deliberately worked' to defeat the 'conciliatory proposals'. War guilt was therefore used to justify the confiscation of resources from Germany but was discreetly buried within the body of the Treaty.

The German perception was the reverse of this. War guilt was the linchpin for every other clause. As such it had to be contested vigorously, partly to discredit all the other provisions and partly because, in the words of Brockdorff-Rantzau, admission would be 'a lie' (Source B). According to Source D, Germany may have made a 'political error' but this was no worse than the actions of the Entente Powers mentioned in Conclusions 1, 13, 14 and 16. The German case was therefore primarily against sole war guilt and in favour of a more collective responsibility.

4

CRISIS AND RECOVERY, 1920–23

BACKGROUND NARRATIVE

The first four years of the Republic's existence were highly problematic. In the first place, the government was confronted by the Versailles settlement, imposed upon it without negotiation; the impact of this was examined in Chapter 3. The Republic also experienced a rapid increase in inflation which, by 1923, had reached unprecedented levels. This was accompanied by problems with the payment of reparations, the final bill for which was announced by the Reparations Commission in 1921. When, in 1923, the Commission declared the German government to be in default on one of the instalments, French troops invaded the Ruhr. This provoked a policy of non-co-operation and passive resistance by the population.

Meanwhile, there had also been a series of political threats. These came from both ends of the political spectrum, the far left and the radical right. In January 1919 the Spartacists, recently reformed as the KPD, tried to seize power in Berlin. At the same time there was a Communist *coup* in Bavaria which resulted momentarily in a Soviet Republic. In 1920 and 1921 there were further disturbances in the Ruhr, Saxony and Thuringia.

The activities of the far right were even more threatening. Fringe groups organised and carried out the assassination of two prominent politicians, Erzberger and Rathenau, and attempted to kill ex-Chancellor Scheidemann. In 1920 Wolfgang Kapp and General Luttwitz attempted to take over Berlin and overthrow the Republic. The government withdrew to Stuttgart and a general strike paralysed the essential services so that Kapp had to give up the attempt. In 1923 Hitler tried to seize control in Munich, intending to take advantage of the financial crisis of the Republic and march on Berlin. This was put down by the Bavarian authorities.

By the end of 1923 the worst was over. The army under von Seeckt had refrained from backing right-wing movements and had taken an active role in putting down left-wing revolts. President Ebert had made effective use of Article 48 of the Constitution and Stresemann introduced a series of economic reforms late in 1923 to restore the finances. These encouraged the involvement of the foreign powers and a package of measures was put together under the Dawes Plan in 1924 to strengthen the German economy and reschedule reparations payments. The way was open for recovery and retrenchment.

ANALYSIS (1): WHY WAS THE REPUBLIC CONFRONTED BY CRISIS BETWEEN 1920 AND 1923?

A crisis is the point in a sequence of events when the future is finely balanced between two or more very different alternatives. It can be sudden, with a swift outcome, or prolonged and exacerbated by uncertainty. The experience of the Weimar Republic was very much the latter: a series of economic and political pressures placed it under considerable strain so that it seemed for much of its first four years of existence to be poised between survival and collapse. During the same period democracy died in Italy, one of the victors of the First World War. The burden of military defeat made Germany additionally vulnerable.

There was unquestionably an economic crisis, with the most extreme bout of inflation ever recorded up until that time. Two sets of figures show the extent of the problem. The first is the exchange rate between the German mark and the US dollar. In 1914 the mark had been valued at 4.2 to the dollar; at the end of the war it stood at 8.9. The decline of the mark accelerated in 1923, by November reaching 42,000,000,000 to the dollar. The second is the rise in the wholesale prices index, from 1 in 1913 to 9.11 in 1921, and 1,261,000,000,000 by December 1923. Only Hungary, at the end of the Second World War, produced more spectacular figures than this. Two principal theories have been advanced as to why this occurred.

One is that it was promoted by external factors. According to Snyder, 'the entire problem was closely connected with the reparations demanded by the Allies.' (1) This, however, is contested by Layton: 'the reparations issue should be seen as a contributory factor to the inflation and not as a primary cause.' (2) Neither view is quite right. Inflation started before reparations became an issue; the connection with reparations cannot therefore be considered 'the entire problem'. Yet reparations were more than merely a 'contributory factor' to the acceleration of inflation. It therefore makes sense to distinguish between the earlier stage, creeping inflation, which was the result of long-term structural problems within the economy and the pressures exerted by war, and the later stage, hyper-inflation, which was directly related to the obligation after 1921 to pay reparations. The connection between the various developments in the reparations saga and the collapse of the mark is too strong to be coincidental. Inflation became hyper-inflation immediately after the announcement of the final amount of 132,000 million gold marks by the Reparations Commission in 1921: the government increased the printing of paper money to buy foreign currency in order to meet its obligations. The climax of hyper-inflation occurred when the Reparations Commission declared Germany in default of one of the payments and the French invaded the Ruhr. The dramatic collapse of the mark was the direct result of this occupation and the passive resistance to it, which caused a severe dislocation of energy supplies to the rest of Germany and necessitated huge imports of coal from abroad – again financed by paper currency.

The second theory is that the German government deliberately provoked the inflationary crisis to avoid paying reparations. The argument here is that the Republican government was both incensed by the announcement of the final sum and afraid of the verdict of the German people should they aim to meet it. Hence they pursued a policy of default, provoking a crisis with the Allies in order to avoid one with the population. Kolb maintains that 'The government's passiveness in the matter of currency stabilization is no doubt to be interpreted as part of its strategy over reparations.' (3) Snyder believes that any such charge is 'incorrect and unjust', especially since 'the process of inflation was already under way when the French occupied the Ruhr'. (4) At most, the action of the German government was unwitting, through the use of deficit spending.

The following is offered as a provisional alternative to both theories. German inflation was caused by a combination of factors which interacted. The war brought about creeping inflation, halving the value of the mark against the dollar. The Berlin government accelerated this by introducing its policy of deficit spending from 1919 onwards. At first this was motivated by domestic concerns: to try to finance reconstruction without placing additional tax burdens on the German people, which would have been the only other possibility. Hence it resorted to a policy of printing notes. Once the Reparations Commission had announced the final bill in 1921 the government had two further considerations. One was the need to find foreign currency to pay the reparations to keep the Allies happy. The other was to avoid transferring the impact of this to the German economy – which would make the German population profoundly unhappy. Deficit financing was the short cut to achieving this equation. The clinching factor was that domestic financial collapse would demonstrate to the Allies in the strongest possible terms the inherent injustice of the reparations terms. Once the French had invaded the Ruhr, there was little incentive to put a stop to the printing presses and the hyper-inflation merged with the government policy of passive resistance. As events turned out, this proved effective in bringing the Allies to their senses.

Accompanying economic instability was a political malaise. This can be seen as an underlying tendency to produce a series of specific crises, all provoked by activists opposing the very existence of the Republic. Political instability was enhanced by the lack of commitment shown to the Republic by the majority of the population (after all, the support for the three parties of the coalition had dropped between 1919 and 1920 from 76.2% to 47.5%) and by open hostility from the radical fringes on the left and right of the political spectrum.

The threat from the far left had already become apparent with the Spartacist revolt in January 1919 and with the emergence of the Bavarian Soviet Republic in April. The intention in each case was nothing short of revolutionary – the creation of a regime modelled on Bolshevik Russia, with a system of soviets to replace the parliamentary regime set up in 1919. The threat may have been contained by the action of the Reichswehr in 1919, but the government continued to see in the left the main danger to the future of the Constitution and liberal democracy. Most subsequent activism indicated profound dis-illusionment among the radical section of the trade union movement – especially with the perceived failure of the SPD to press for social as well as political change in 1919. A sizeable minority of the working class was therefore attracted to syndicalism, or the use of the strike for political purposes, and to the more holistic concepts of Communism. Challenges came in 1920 from rail and miners' strikes, mass demonstrations by the USPD and uprisings in the Ruhr from a variety of groups, ranging from workers' self-defence units, USPD activists, syndicalists and Communists. 1921 saw Communist revolts in Merseburg, Halle and Mansfeld while, in September and October, Saxony and Thuringia were similarly affected. The situation in Saxony was potentially the most dangerous since it involved a degree of co-operation between the KPD and the SPD Prime Minister of Saxony, Zeigner. It might have created a broad anti-Republican front at state government level and driven a wedge into the national organisation of the SPD.

The threat from the far right, meanwhile, was directly related to German surrender at the end of 1918, to the establishment of the Republic and to the signing of the Treaty of Versailles. It comprised a complete range of action. One form was a policy of total non-co-operation from the DNVP in the Reichstag, which put severe pressure on the moderate parties. Another was the right-wing counterpart to left-wing revolution. The Kapp Putsch of 1920 was potentially lethal. Resisting the dissolution of the Ehrhardt Brigade, ordered by the government in compliance with the Treaty of Versailles, Kapp and Lüttwitz seized power in Berlin. What made this particularly dangerous was that the army itself took no action against Kapp, despite being ordered to do so by President Ebert. Less dramatic, although more significant, was the overthrow of constitutional government in Bavaria and the assumption of emergency powers by Kahr in 1922. A haven was thereby created for disaffected right-wing groups, the most important of which was the Nazi movement. This attempted the most radical move of all in the 1923 Munich Putsch, the inspiration for which came directly from Mussolini's 'March on Rome' the year before. Like Italy, Germany was threatened by Fascism as well as by Communism.

Right-wing activism also included political terrorism, which added greatly to the climate of unrest and sustained the impression of a crisis. Prominent victims included government ministers. Erzberger was a target partly because he had headed the German peace delegation and had been in favour of signing the Treaty, and partly because he was the linchpin holding together the coalition of the Centre, DDP and SPD. His death, it was thought, would cause the collapse of consensus and with it the Republic itself. When this did not have the desired effect, Rathenau, the Foreign Minister, was torn to pieces by machine-gunfire and a hand grenade in June 1922, a method calculated to have a sensational impact on the public.

The convergence of international pressure, economic instability and hostility from both political wings would have been enough to test any regime. Kolb maintains that it was 'almost a miracle that the Weimar democracy succeeded in maintaining its existence during these years of extreme tribulation'. (5) Or was it?

Questions

1. 'There was no crisis facing the Weimar Republic between 1920 and 1923, only individual crises.' Do you agree?
2. Were the problems confronting the government between 1920 and 1923 self-inflicted?

ANALYSIS (2): WHY HAD THE REPUBLIC NOT COLLAPSED BY 1923?

At first sight it is strange that the Weimar Republic should have survived its first crisis (1919–23), and perished in its second (1929–33) for which it ought to have been better prepared. There are, however, perfectly feasible explanations for this, based on the premise that the situation in the early 1920s was superficially more threatening but fundamentally less destabilising than that in the early 1930s. This theme is completed in Chapter 7.

The early attempts to overthrow the Republic were spectacular, but they lacked the necessary overall co-ordination to succeed. The radical left never accounted for more than 15% of electoral support in the polls. Its bids for power in Berlin, Bavaria, the Ruhr, Saxony and Thuringia were short-lived, partly because they fell between two stools: they lacked the professional and conspiratorial organisation of the Bolsheviks without becoming a large enough mass movement to generate overwhelming spontaneous support. In any case, most of the support of the working class went consistently to the SPD, which had an extensive trade union infrastructure committed to evolutionary change rather than to syndicalism or revolution. All the KPD succeeded in doing was to make itself the main target of the government and, with the one exception of Saxony, prevent any possibility of reconciliation with the SPD.

The government's preoccupation with the left probably enhanced the opportunities of the right, but even these were not fully exploited.

The far right was fragmented into small völkisch groups which often competed against each other. It was not until the late 1920s that they had been absorbed into a more homogeneous Nazi movement. In the early 1920s, too, the far right lacked the full co-operation of the conservative right. The DNVP remained suspicious of some of the groups, partly because of their social origins within the lumpenproletariat. Hence, although they sympathised with their hatred of the Republic and everything it stood for, they were reluctant to be drawn into what seemed at this stage to be hair-brained schemes for a change of regime. In the case of Bavaria the conservative right took direct action against the Nazis. Kahr was entirely unconvinced about Hitler's proposal to march on Berlin. It was because he withheld his support that Hitler tried to seize the beer hall in which Kahr was addressing a meeting. Hitler's failure was due at least in part to Kahr aligning himself with the establishment, even if that establishment meant the Republic. This was a major contrast with the action of the conservative right, especially the DNVP, after 1929: suspicion was replaced by close co-operation between them and the Nazis.

There is another factor which helped the Republic survive before 1923. The far right was perceived as thuggish and undisciplined and, although many of its adherents came from the Freikorps, it did not as yet have the support of the army leadership. It is true that von Seeckt did not take action against Kapp in 1920, but he did not provide any help either. The army was therefore poised uncertainly between resistance to and support for the Republic and at this stage it was only fringe sections of the Freikorps that were directly subversive or violent. Later, the army was to find a more comfortable role within the broader right, especially with Hindenburg as President and commander-in-chief, and Schleicher as Chancellor. Von Seeckt even acted as a moderating influence over Bavaria; although sympathetic to Kahr, he advised him strongly not to involve himself in far right-wing activities, which probably played an important part in Kahr's decision not to go along with Hitler's putsch. Because of these disparate attitudes, the right was therefore not ready to take over from the Republic in 1923. Ten years later it was.

Despite their aggression, the two political fringes found it difficult to persuade the bulk of the population in the early 1920s that another change of regime was necessary. Nor, at this stage, did they have a charismatic personality capable of breaking through this psychological barrier. The two successful examples of mass action were those mobilised by the government in 1920 and 1923. In the first, the SPD made effective use of its trade union infrastructure to organise a strike of workers in essential industries in Berlin. The result was that the Kapp Putsch collapsed, unable to govern without electricity, gas, transportation and water. The second, a campaign of civil disobedience, had the similar effect of making it impossible for the French to impose effective military occupation over the Ruhr. It seemed that in the early 1920s mass-mobilisation was still the prerogative of the forces maintaining the status quo, not of those trying to disrupt it.

This brings us to the firm action taken by the government against threats of disruption. President Ebert made full use of the emergency powers available to him under Article 48 of the Constitution to deal with the Kapp and Munich Putsches on the right and with the Spartacist, Ruhr and Saxon threats on the left. In the last of these examples, the government declared a state of national emergency. Part of the process involved the transfer of political power to regional military commanders under orders from the Ministry of Defence in Berlin. The Prime Minister of Saxony, Zeigner, was removed from office when he refused to co-operate and the threatened Communist insurgency was soon mopped up by army detachments and the police. It could therefore be argued that the early history of Article 48 helped to save the Republic, just as its later history was a significant factor in its destruction.

The Chancellorship was also used effectively, especially at the height of the crisis in 1923. Gustav Stresemann was prepared to take a pragmatic and tough line which extricated Germany remarkably quickly from economic collapse. Making the most of presidential support, he imposed the necessary cuts in government expenditure and introduced strict budgetary controls. He also delegated to Schacht and Luther the task of replacing the devalued currency with the Rentenmark, which was given equal value to the pre-war gold Reichsmark. The proposal was massively ambitious, requiring considerable confidence and, it has to be said, a degree of chance and even bluff. The new Rentenmark was based on land values, which meant in effect that 'the German people mortgaged their entire personal resources as coverage for the new mark'. (6) This actually proved highly successful in winning the western powers round to the view that Germany deserved their support in her search for rehabilitation.

Finally, there were certain external factors favouring the Republic in 1924. The right-wing government of Poincaré had given way to a more moderate one which was prepared to pull French troops out of the Ruhr. The year 1924 also saw the first Labour government in Britain under the leadership of Ramsay MacDonald who saw it as his main role to restore harmony to Europe. The result was the Dawes Plan of

1924 which put forward a package of proposals to restore normality to Germany, including the evacuation of the Ruhr, a phasing of reparations payments according to an index of prosperity, and the provision of loans by the United States. In return, Germany undertook to share control over reparations payments with seven foreign representatives in a central bank of issue, while an American financier would be appointed as an Agent General of Reparations Payments. Although these terms caused resentment in some quarters, they nevertheless underpinned domestic efforts to restore financial solvency and the investment side of the Plan provided the foundation for prosperity between 1924 and 1929.

The crises between 1919 and 1923 were insufficient to destroy the Republic at this stage. The radical left and right were disunited and the role of the army was ambivalent. The government was able to use the constitution to keep control, while efforts to rehabilitate the finances were seen by other powers as a sign that external assistance was now necessary. By the time of the next crisis all this had changed. In the meantime, however, survival was followed by recovery and consolidation during the so-called 'Stresemann era'.

Questions

1. Did the Weimar Republic 'save itself' between 1919 and 1923?
2. 'The fact that the Weimar Republic survived between 1920 and 1923 shows that it did not face a crisis at all.' Do you agree?

SOURCES

1. WHAT MOTIVATED POLITICAL ACTION?

Source A: Kapp's proclamation to the German people, 13 March 1920.

The hour to rescue Germany has been lost. There remains only a government of action.

What are our tasks?

The government will fulfil its obligations under the peace treaty, in so far as it does not violate the honour and the life of the German people . . .

The government stands for economic freedom . . .

The government will ruthlessly suppress strikes and sabotage. Strikes mean treason to the people, the Fatherland, and the future.

This will not be a government of one-sided capitalism, but it will defend German labour against the harsh fate of international slavery under finance capitalism . . .

The government regards it as its most holy duty to protect the war wounded and widows of our fallen fighters.

Source B: a nationalist song, published in the *Social Democrat*.

Let us happy be and gay
Smash Wirth's skull until it crack
Happy, tra-la-la,
Soon the Kaiser will be back!
When the Kaiser's home again
We'll cripple Wirth to his great pain;
The rifles shall stutter, tack, tack, tack,
On the Red rascals and the Black.

Beat, beat Wirth, beat him black and blue
Smash his skull till his brains come through;
Shoot down Walter Rathenau
The Goddamned swine of a Jewish sow.

Source C: from Hitler's speech at his trial in Munich, February 1924.

The fate of Germany does not lie in the choice between a Republic or a Monarchy, but in the content of the Republic and the Monarchy. What I am contending against is not the form of a state as such, but its ignominious content. We wanted to create in Germany the precondition which alone will make it possible for the iron grip of our enemies to be removed from us. We wanted to create order in the state, throw out the drones, take up the fight against international stock exchange slavery, against our whole economy being cornered by trusts, against the politicising of trade unions, and above all, for the highest honourable duty which we, as Germans, know should be once more introduced – the duty of bearing arms, military service. And now I ask you: Is what we wanted high treason?

Questions

1. Who were 'Kapp' (Source A) and 'Wirth' (Source B)? [2]
2. What are the main similarities and contrasts between Sources A and C? How would you explain these? [5]
3. Comment on the differences in type between Sources A to C. [5]
*4. What reasons would you suggest for the publication of Source B in the *Social Democrat*? [6]
5. Using Sources A to C, and your own knowledge, explain why attempts were made to overthrow the Weimar Republic. [7]

Worked answer

*4. The *Social Democrat* was the main political mouthpiece of the SPD and would not have published any material unless it was seen to be of advantage to that party.

By publishing a nationalist song, with all its violent language, the newspaper intended to elicit disgust from its readers and to confirm their support for the SPD and its coalition partners. It could not fail to have immediate impact: most people would be immediately outraged by the violent references to 'smashing skulls', spilling brains and beating 'black and blue'.

Discriminating readers would also spot the underlying right-wing prejudices contained within the song. The reference to the Kaiser being 'home again' would convey a warning of resurgent monarchism, while the phrase 'rifles shall stutter' gave clear indication of paramilitary activism. The descriptions 'Red rascals and the Black' referred to the socialists of the SPD and the clerical influences of the Centre: since the two parties were in coalition, no harm could be done by publicising this double insult. Finally, there was a blatant anti-Semitic reference in 'Goddamned swine of a Jewish sow'. The *Social Democrat* was using such doggerel in a subtle way as part of a propaganda offensive against the whole of the right, including the DNVP.

SOURCES

2. THE IMPACT OF ECONOMIC CRISIS

Source D: Evidence provided for German default by the Reparations Commission, 26 December 1922.
[See figure 3]

Category of timber	Amount ordered	Contracts made by German Government	Per cent	Amount due on 30th Sept.	Amount received in Germany by French Agents at 30th Sept.	Per cent of the order	Dispatched	Per cent of the order
Sawn Wood	53,000	54,935	100	55,000	17,417	31.5	15,950	29
Telegraph Poles	200,000	75,694	38	145,000	46,133	23.0	40,047	20

Figure 3 Evidence provided for German default by the Reparations Commission, 26 December 1922

Source: L. L. Snyder: *The Weimar Republic* (Princeton, NJ 1966), Reading 24.

Source E: Wholesale Prices Index 1913–23, rounded to nearest whole number (1913=1).

1913	1
1918	2
1919	4
1920	15
1921	19
1922	342
1923 (Jan)	2783
1923 (Dec)	1,261,000,000,000

Source F: from the Diary of Lord D'Abernon, British Ambassador to Berlin (published in 1929), Berlin, 11 August 1922.

One of the comedy-tragedy episodes of the visit of the Committee of Guarantees to Berlin was the payment by the German Government of their railway expenses, including their special car, which waited here six weeks. This was done in 20-mark notes, and it required seven office boys with huge waste-paper-baskets full of these notes to carry the full sum from the office down to the railway station.

Source G: a personal memoir from Dr Frieda Wunderlich.

An acquaintance of mine, a clergyman, came to Berlin from a suburb with his monthly salary to buy a pair of shoes for his baby; he could buy only a cup of coffee.

Source H: from a speech by Franz Bumm, President of the Department of Health, to the Reichstag, 20 February 1923.

The height to which prices have climbed may be shown by the fact that as of February 15, wholesale prices have risen on the average to 5967 times the peacetime level, those of foodstuffs to 4902 times, and those for industrial products to 7958 times . . . For many people, meat has become altogether a rarity. A million and a half German families are inadequately provided with fuel. Thousands upon thousands of people spend their lives jammed together in the most primitive dwellings and must wait for years before they can be assigned quarters which satisfy even the most elementary hygienic requirements. It is understandable that under such unhygienic circumstances, health levels are deteriorating ever more seriously . . . After having fallen in 1920–21, it [the mortality rate] has climbed again for the year 1921–22, rising from 12.6 to 13.4 per thousand inhabitants. In 1922 those familiar diseases appeared again in increasing numbers which attack a people when it is suffering from insufficient nutrition, when it also can no longer obtain the other necessities of life. Thus edema is reappearing, the so-called war dropsy, which is a consequence of a bad and overly watery diet. There are increases in stomach disorders and food poisoning, which are the result of eating spoiled foods. There are complaints of the reappearance of scurvy, which is a consequence of an unbalanced and improper diet.

Questions

1. Explain the references to 'Reparations Commission' (Source D) and 'Wolesale Prices Index' (Source E). [4]
2. How strong was the evidence in Source D as a justification for the French invasion of the Ruhr in January 1923? [5]
3. Does Source E show that Germany's inflation was due primarily to the French invasion of the Ruhr? [5]
*4. Of what value are Sources F and G to the historian studying the impact of inflation on Germany? Is one more reliable than the other? [5]
5. Was the speaker in Source H correct in attributing to inflation all the problems to which he referred? Use the other Sources and your own knowledge. [6]

Worked answer

*4. Both Sources F and G are primary sources of the type used by historians as evidence for the actual impact of hyper-inflation on the population. They help to translate into real terms the astronomical figures shown in Source D. From them can also be inferred differing attitudes, according to the position of the observer. The British Ambassador, for example, offered a more detached observation on a 'tragedy-comedy' episode, while Dr Frieda Wunderlich showed a more direct personal involvement. Each account therefore represents a microcosm of social history which some historians would prefer to the mainstream of political and economic developments.

There is little to choose between the two sources in terms of reliability. Both use anecdotal evidence of the experiences of others. In Source F the process of transmission could have been more involved, thereby increasing the chances of distortion or exaggeration, whereas the experience of the subject of Source G is simpler and less liable to embellishment. Offset against this, the memoir (Source G) is likely to be a less immediate record than a diary (Source F), which usually involves an entry while the memory of an event is fresh. Both stories are, however, entirely plausible within the context of the hyper-inflation of 1923, as there are many others like them.

5

A PERIOD OF STABILITY, 1924–29?

BACKGROUND NARRATIVE

The period between 1924 and 1929 is usually considered to have been the most affluent and stable in the history of the Weimar Republic. Certainly there were no major attempts at revolutionary change and the economy seemed to recover steadily after the hyper-inflation of 1921–23.

The economy was underpinned in 1924 by the Dawes Plan which rescheduled Germany's reparations payments and spread the load according to an index of prosperity. The process was taken further when the Young Plan (1929) extended the deadline for final payment to 58 years. Meanwhile, American loans were vital for the expansion of German industry, which benefited from new industrial techniques from the United States – an influence generally known as Fordism. The government did what it could to foster greater prosperity by channelling investment into industry and public works schemes, increasing welfare benefits and encouraging more positive industrial relations through compulsory arbitration in the event of disputes between workers and management.

Administrations continued to be based entirely on coalitions, the mainstay of which were the Centre Party. Their leader, Marx, was Chancellor between November 1923 and January 1925 and between May 1926 and June 1928. The SPD were not involved in any of the governments between 1924 and 1928. This was partly through choice, as they tended to criticise the domestic policies of the Centre and DVP. At the end of the period, however, the SPD returned to power, joining the Centre, DDP and DVP. The period ended as it had begun, with a grand coalition.

ANALYSIS (1): HOW 'STABLE' WAS THE WEIMAR REPUBLIC ECONOMICALLY BETWEEN 1924 AND 1929?

The usual argument is that the economy of the Weimar Republic went through three main stages – two of which might be seen as 'negative' and one as 'positive'. The first of the 'negative periods' (1919–23) was one of inflation, becoming hyper-inflation after 1921. The second 'negative period' was the depression from 1929 onwards, which resulted in a massive rise in unemployment and the collapse of Germany's production figures. Between the two periods there were six years of economic recovery, often seen as the 'golden age' of the Weimar Republic, in which the economy went through a boom before the crisis of 1929. There are two quite different perspectives on this interpretation.

At one level there is much to be said for seeing 1924–29 as a period of rapid economic recovery. Under the initial influence of the Dawes Plan (1924), the sting was drawn from the commitment to reparations payments and an enormous boost was provided by the inflow of investments from the United States. These were used to finance industrial expansion and a variety of public works schemes, including sports stadia, swimming pools, huge apartment blocks and opera houses – all of which provided employment and enabled the government to fulfil the sort of role advocated by Keynesian economists. There could also be more extensive investment in social and welfare services and an increase in wages for state employees. Prosperity was therefore an experience shared by the population as a whole.

German industries made the most of the American connection, more than doubling their overall production between 1923 and 1929. Firms made extensive use of innovative techniques, which were influenced by 'Fordism' from the United States, and by experimental methods of scientific management. According to Snyder, the Germans 'mastered the lessons of mass production, including the standardization of patterns, interchangeable parts, improved methods of accounting, and advertising designed to promote sales and distribution.' (1) The

American example enabled Germany to produce an industrial hybrid which was far more effective than the British production model; the latter was largely dependent on traditional technology and industrial methods.

Industrial efficiency was also enhanced by the development of the cartel system, the purpose of which was to develop co-operation rather than excessive competition between the great industrial enterprises. These cartels included Vereinigte Stahlwerke and I.G. Farben, the latter controlling some 400 firms. Again, there was a marked contrast with the smaller-scale organisation of British industry. Complementing efficiency from above was the prospect of harmony with the workforce below – in marked contrast to the British experience of the general strike in 1926. The Weimar Constitution had envisaged a new industrial partnership. Under Article 165, 'Workers and employees are called upon to cooperate, on an equal footing, with employers in the regulation of wages and of the conditions of labour, as well as in the general development of productive forces.' (2) After 1923 the government played a more active role in this by imposing compulsory arbitration over disputes between workers and management, thus reducing the number of strikes.

By this analysis, therefore, the German economy was in a strong position. According to Bookbinder, 'By 1929 Germany had become the world's second industrial power behind the United States. Real wages rose, and the standard of living for many increased dramatically.' (3) The corollary to this is that any real threat to Germany's economic stability would be external, not internal. Snyder sees the essential cause of 'the next economic crisis' in 'the world depression of 1929', which 'hit Germany with tremendous impact'. (4) There is, however, a danger in this approach. It sees economic collapse as monocausal. There must be an alternative perspective. If the Depression which followed the Wall Street Crash exercised such a profound impact on the German economy, there must have been a faultline within that economy.

The answer could be that the recovery after 1923 was based far too heavily on externally generated credit. American investments were bound to be highly attractive since they offered an easy alternative to having to increase domestic taxation. They were also used in a dangerous way. Short-term loans were used to finance long-term capital projects, the assumption being that it would not be difficult to renew the loans as payments fell due. This made Germany highly vulnerable to any major fluctuation on the American stock market; following the Wall Street Crash most short-term loans were recalled.

This explanation is enough to satisfy some historians. The German economy was sound apart from this one flaw – the one which, in the circumstances, proved fatal. But can we agree even with this? We still have a monocausal analysis: a single external factor reacting with a single source of internal vulnerability. What we can actually see in retrospect is a series of flaws and contradictions within the economy.

The whole basis of Germany's industrial performance between 1924 and 1929, successful though it seemed to be on the surface, was fundamentally unsound – because it was inherently out of balance. Increased production did not translate into enlarged volumes of foreign trade. The consumer demand would therefore have to come from within Germany. But between 1928 and 1929 capital goods production rose by 2% while, at the same time, consumer goods production dropped back by 3%. (5) The industrial drive was not, therefore, consumer-based. Hence there was a rapid increase in industrial capacity, inspired by Fordism and American techniques of mass production, which could not be fully used. The decline of Britain's staple industries in the 1920s provided a warning of what could happen in any recession, let alone a slump the size of that which hit the world in 1929.

Within this context, the development of cartels cannot be seen automatically as an advantage. These carved up the market between them and arranged prices which were often detrimental to the consumer. Competition might have driven down prices and hence enlarged the domestic market. The cartelisation of German industry may have been accompanied by American production methods but, as Berghahn points out, 'without subscribing to the American idea that the introduction of mass production would reduce prices and thus also benefit the mass of the population'. (6) Faced with a limited consumer potential they took refuge increasingly in the non-consumer industries which had been their original base. This, in turn, had political implications as, at the end of the 1920s they began to see their salvation in rearmament. It is therefore hardly surprising that they became anti-progressive, anti-Republican and strongly supportive of the political right.

The result was the alienation of the workforce. Although there were fewer strikes between 1924 and 1929 than in the first few years of the Weimar Republic, this does not necessarily mean that there was greater industrial harmony. Expectations among wage-earners were bound to increase, especially since the bout of inflation up until 1923 had depleted their capital. As it was, increased wages did little more than keep pace with the rising cost of living. There was therefore plenty of cause for industrial dispute. The number of days lost through strikes was kept down only through government intervention. Although conceived in highly positive terms, this had two unforeseen side-effects. The first was that compulsory government arbitration in disputes drove the cartels into an increasingly rigid and authoritarian stance with the workforce – and further co-operation with each other to defend the flawed status quo. The second effect was that the expanding role of the state in introducing the eight-hour working day and expanding welfare benefits was bound to put pressure on economic expansion and to create conflicts of opinion as to where the new wealth should go. Industrialists argued for recycling profits into increased industrial production, but, as we have seen, this would only have met with saturated markets. Trade unionists gave priority to social investment and higher wages, but this only served to reduce the cost-effectiveness of existing production, making large-scale cut-backs in employment inevitable in any prolonged recession. Indeed, Germany was especially vulnerable to high levels of unemployment. Although there had been a decrease from 2 million unemployed in 1926 to 1.4 million in 1928, the number had crept up to 1.9 million by 1929, before the impact of the slump was actually felt.

Finally, there was one sector of the economy that had been largely unaffected even by the brief period of prosperity which had existed. Agriculture had consistently proved to be one of the weaker points of the German economy. Affected by the growing competitiveness between agricultural producers across the world, the German farmers needed to modernise in the same way that German industrialists had been prepared to do. But modernisation never really reached the farms and estates, most of the investments bypassing them altogether. The result was that agricultural production was more haphazard than industrial output during the period of prosperity, actually falling back in 1926. It is significant that those engaged in farming were to be politically radicalised even before the onset of depression: they could be seen as a barometer for things to come.

Overall, the economy of the Weimar Republic did recover between 1924 and 1929, but this recovery was highly fragile. It will not do, therefore, to say that external forces in 1929 wrecked a thriving system. They brought down one which was struggling to find an internal equilibrium between a series of conflicting developments. The German economy was living on borrowed time as well as on borrowed money.

Questions

1. Was the period 1924–29 a recovery from the economic crisis of 1921–23 or a preparation for the crisis of 1929–33?
2. How well did governments manage Germany's economy between 1924 and 1929?

ANALYSIS (2): HOW 'STABLE' WAS THE WEIMAR REPUBLIC POLITICALLY BETWEEN 1924 AND 1929?

As with the Weimar economy, the political system between 1924 and 1929 appears to have been generally stable. Further investigation, however, shows that this was partly illusory.

Evidence can be produced to support the argument for political recovery and consolidation. From 1924 there were no further attempts to overthrow the Republic to compare with the Spartacist uprising (1919), the Kapp Putsch (1920) and the Munich Putsch (1923). The electoral performance of the parties hostile to the Republic seemed to be in decline, both on the left and on the right. This is supported by comparing the Reichstag elections of May 1924 and May 1928, when the KPD declined from 62 seats to 54, the DNVP from 95 to 73 and the Nazis from 32 to 12. In the same elections the parties supporting the Republic either held steady or increased their representation. The SPD were up from 100 to 153, the Centre moved from 64 to 62 and the DDP from 28 to 25, while the DVP remained unaltered on 45. Overall, the radical parties fell from 187 seats to 149, while the moderate parties increased from 237 to 285. The differential between the two groups widened from 50 to 136: this can surely be seen as statistical confirmation of political stability.

To strengthen this impression, the last years of the period saw the revival of the grand coalition of the first years, a broad collaboration between the SPD, Centre, DDP and DVP, under the leadership of Müller. It has often been argued that the grand coalition fell because of the impact of the Depression which brought about a break in 1930, between Müller and the SPD on the one hand and Brüning and the Centre on the other, over the specific question of unemployment benefits. This was followed by the increasingly authoritarian regime of Brüning and his use of presidential powers under Article 48 of the Constitution. The Depression in other words destroyed the most promising political combination of the whole period, cutting short political recovery and reversing the apparent decline of the Nazis and DNVP.

However, there is an alternative perspective. The 'positive period' between 1924 and 1929 can actually be seen as a negative one. Electoral statistics are incomplete in that they do not show the political tensions which were steadily building up and which broke through the surface after 1929. They do not show the breakdown of political consensus and the fragmentation of that part of the spectrum which supported the Republic. Nor do they hint at the greater cohesion of the right, the main threat to the Republic's institutions.

Just because the moderate parties consolidated their electoral support did not automatically guarantee political stability. The real difficulty came not so much in getting a majority between them in the Reichstag, but rather in transforming that majority into a stable government. The multiplicity of parties and the use of proportional representation meant that all governments were coalitions. Unfortunately, the aims and policies of the individual parties made it difficult to achieve a large-scale coalition which would at the same time be stable. The SPD, for example, refused to serve in any coalition containing members of the DNVP. Hence the only real alternatives were a coalition from moderate left to moderate right consisting of the SPD, DDP, Centre and DVP, or a coalition from centre to right, comprising DDP, Centre, DVP and DNVP, a so-called 'bourgeois bloc'. The moderate combination worked reasonably well when it came to foreign policy but tended to fracture on domestic policy, when Reichstag majorities had to be manufactured for each item of legislation. The 'bourgeois bloc' would not work for foreign policy, particularly since the DNVP opposed Stresemann's policy of *détente* in Europe – hence in this instance there had to be majorities negotiated for individual treaties. According to Peukert, 'There was something unnatural about all these political permutations, since deep-seated regional tensions and ideological differences had to be glossed over for the sake of making the parliamentary arithmetic come out right, and there was no real meeting of minds on political goals.' (7)

Part of the reason for this was that the differences between the parties was widening throughout the so-called period of recovery. The SPD were moving further to the left, emphasising their trade union connections and their underlying commitment to expanding the scope of welfare policies. This was enough to keep them out of government between 1924 and 1928. The Centre Party, by contrast, was tending more to the *laissez-faire* view of the right, a process accelerated by the leadership first of Monsignor Kaas, then of Heinrich Brüning. This made it easier for the Centre to relate, in domestic issues, to the DNVP than to the SPD. The liberal parties, meanwhile, were far more vulnerable than their electoral performance suggests. The DVP was always ambivalent about the Republic and it was really only Stresemann's personal influence which held some of its members within the coalitions. As for the DDP, it was rapidly losing its role: it no longer saw its main purpose as to uphold individual 'freedom to' and it was not converted to the SPD's more welfare-based 'freedom from'. Despite their showing in 1928, the liberal parties were on the point of breaking up, which explains the suddenness of their collapse in 1930.

Accompanying this divisiveness of party politics was a growing disillusionment with what they actually represented. This was articulated by Stresemann, who did more than most to try to keep inter-party co-operation going. 'We must demand that the spirit of party be confined to what is vitally required for Germany's development, that Parliament itself exert the pressure to produce a real and not merely formal majority.' (8) Gustav Stolper, a member of the DDP, went even further: 'What we have today,' he said in 1929, 'is a coalition of ministers, not a coalition of parties. There are no government parties, only opposition parties. This state of things is a greater danger to the democratic system than ministers and parliamentarians realize.' (9)

All these problems were converging within the grand coalition by 1929. The traditional argument is that this coalition broke up in 1930 on the issue of cutting unemployment benefits; this, in turn was the direct result of the Depression which transformed an economic crisis into a political one. This is only partly true. The parties of the grand coalition were already divided over welfare policies generally and had sharpened their views since 1924. By 1929 The Centre and DVP were already in broad agreement with a memorandum issued by industrial leaders. Entitled *Progress or Decline*, this demanded reduced taxation and lower social benefits, which should, in any case, be made available only to those in real need of them. The social benefit system should therefore be fundamentally reorganised. The SPD, by contrast, insisted that welfare provision should actually be extended. Hence, according to Kolb, 'The "great coalition" did not break up on account of a fractional alteration in the rate of unemployment insurance contributions; it foundered on a basic issue of social policy, in which all the potential for domestic conflict was concentrated in 1930.' Or, to put it another way, the coalition fractured along the fault line which had appeared before 1929.

At the same time, there had been a gradual strengthening of the anti-Republican forces of the right. Appearances are deceptive here. The figures, as we have seen, show a decline in their electoral performance. But what these figures do not reveal is a fundamental realignment of the right as it moved into position for the onslaught on the Republic after 1930; any loss of support which accompanied this repositioning was only temporary. Four major changes were involved.

The first was a complete overhaul of the NSDAP. The Party was given a monolithic structure which enhanced Hitler's control through the unit of the regional *Gau*, each under the authority of a *Gauleiter*. There was also a revised strategy for achieving power. The failure of the Munich Putsch had shown that violence alone was unlikely to succeed; the best course would therefore be to participate in regular politics in order to achieve power constitutionally. Once this had been achieved, the revolution could be imposed from above. The new approach gradually established the NSDAP as a mainstream and respectable party which, in turn, began to attract a proportion of the middle classes. At first this was limited, as was demonstrated by the poor showing in the 1928 election. It is, however, significant that Hitler had already made contact with the needs of the rural middle classes well before the onset of the Depression in 1929.

The second change affecting the right was the radicalisation of the DNVP, which occurred at the same time as the Nazi quest for respectability. The latter was strongly opposed to the constant inter-vention of the government to arbitrate over disputes between workers and management. They increasingly associated Weimar democracy with a workforce which was fast slipping out of control. What was needed was an authoritarian political system which would recognise the need for greater industrial discipline. The election of Hugenberg as leader in 1929 took the Party further to the right. Like many other politicians, he was disillusioned with the system of party politics but, unlike the moderates of the Centre, DVP and DDP, he saw the solution in the end of party politics and the creation of a broad anti-Republican front.

This brings us to the third change. The Nazi search for respectability and the Nationalist conversion to frontism brought the two right-wing parties together as natural allies. The 1928 elections occurred too early to register the effect of this but by 1929 it had become clear that the most cohesive coalition was not the government but the opposition. The two parties co-operated closely in opposing the Young Plan (1929) and went on to campaign jointly for the election of 1931. Already by 1929 Hugenberg had placed his newspaper chain at Hitler's disposal for the dissemination of Nazi propaganda, an important factor in enhancing the respectability of the far right.

By 1929, therefore, a more cohesive right was emerging to challenge an increasingly fractured coalition. There was one final ingredient which enabled the right to make rapid progress after 1930. This was the rise of President Hindenburg, again something which had occurred during the period of 'stability'. The real significance of Hindenburg's election in 1925 was not immediately apparent. Indeed, Stresemann, normally very astute politically, made an uncharacteristic error of judgement in supporting his candidature. At first Hindenburg seemed genuine in his promise to uphold the Weimar Constitution. Nevertheless, he instinctively disliked the democratic process and it would not take much for him to tolerate the use of Article 48 as a regular rather than extraordinary measure. After 1929 this was to be the device whereby the party politics of the Republic were to fade into insignificance and the right was to have its chance to create an authoritarian alternative.

Overall, there is much to be said for Layton's view that 'the parliamentary and party system had failed to make any real progress in this middle period. It had merely coped.' (10) As with the economy, 'coping' was not enough. There was no resilience to deal with crisis when it came. The usual argument is that economic crisis in 1929 led to political crisis in 1930. In other words, external events impacted upon a reasonable internal stability. It now looks as though that stability had worn through by 1929 and that the collapse of parliamentary politics in 1929 was as much an economic issue proving the last straw in a political situation as it was a political failure caused by an economic crisis.

Questions

1. 'Nothing changed in the pattern of party politics after 1924.' Do you agree?
2. Were the threats to democracy greater between 1924 and 1929 than they had been between 1919 and 1923?

SOURCES

1. ECONOMIC STABILITY?

Source A: Index of German industrial production 1913–30 (1913=100).

1913	100
1919	38
1920	55
1921	66
1922	72
1923	47
1924	70
1925	83
1926	80
1927	100
1928	103
1929	104
1930	91

Source B: Index of exports and imports by volume (1913=100).

	Exports	Imports
1913	100	100
1925	66.4	82.3
1930	92.2	86.0
1932	55.6	62.5

Source C: Unemployment in Germany.

	No. (000s)	% of working population
1913	348	3.0
1921	346	1.8
1922	215	1.1
1923	818	4.1
1924	927	4.9
1925	682	3.4
1926	2,025	10.0
1927	1,312	6.2
1928	1,391	6.3
1929	1,899	8.5
1930	3,076	14.0
1931	4,520	21.9

Source D: Indices of cost of living and workers' wages (1928=100).

	Cost of living	Real wages
1913	66	93
1925	93	81
1926	93	84
1927	97	89
1928	100	100
1929	101	102
1930	97	97
1931	89	94

Source E: Number of strikes and lock-outs.

	Strikes	Working days lost (in 000s)
1913	2464	11,761
1919	3719	33,083
1920	3807	16,755
1921	4485	25,784
1922	4755	27,734
1923	2046	12,344
1924	1973	36,198
1925	1708	2936
1926	351	1222
1927	844	6144
1928	739	20,339
1929	429	4251
1930	353	4029

Source F: The views of Otto Bauer (a Marxist) on the influence of American production methods on Germany, 1931.

Rationalization created its own market. Since the whole of German industry was being renovated technologically, since new plants were being installed and the old reorganized, and new machines were being put to work, the demand for building materials, machines, tools, and steel was very high. The branches of industry specializing in the means of production experienced brisk sales. Since they employed more workers at better wages, the market for those industries producing consumer goods also expanded. Thus was the economic crisis following the stabilization of the mark overcome in 1926. The years 1926 to 1928 were the years of the great rationalization boom . . .

But the rationalization boom necessarily came to a speedy end. As soon as the majority of enterprises were finished renovating their plants technologically, the process of technological adaptation had to proceed more slowly. The slowing down caused the demand for manufactured goods to fall, confronting the industries with stagnation. In turn, the layoff of large numbers of workers led to a downturn in the consumer-goods industry. Thus in 1929 a severe economic crisis set in. Following the rationalization boom came the rationalization crisis.

Questions

1. What agreement, drawn up in 1924, made it possible for United States investments to enter Germany? Name one other effect of this agreement. [3]
2. Do Sources A, C and D show that the German people were better off in 1928 than they had been in 1925? [5]
3. What other types of source would help the historian to show whether or not the German people were better off in 1928 than they had been in 1925? [4]
*4. 'Between 1924 and 1929 there was a considerable improvement in relations between employers and workers.' To what extent does Source E prove this? [5]
5. To what extent is the argument in Source F supported by the evidence in Sources A to E? Use your own knowledge to supplement your answer. [8]

Worked answer

*4. On the surface it does appear that there was an improvement in relations between employers and workers through a reduction in industrial conflict. According to Source E, the number of strikes and lock-outs steadily declined from 1924 to 1926, rose in 1927 but dropped back again in 1928 and 1929. At no time did the number of strikes in any year between 1924 and 1929 approach those typical of the earlier period 1919–23.

These figures are, however, deceptive. The number of strikes does not always reflect the number of working days lost. More significant than the relatively small number of 739 strikes in 1928 is the number of working days lost: at 20,339,000 these actually exceed the equivalent figures for 1920 and 1923, while the total working days lost in 1924 is the largest number on the entire list. The possible explanation for this is that, although fewer in number after 1924, strikes tended to be more disruptive when they did occur. Government intervention to impose arbitration tended to keep down the number of strikes but this did not always work, as with the particularly bitter confrontation in the Ruhr steel industry in 1928. There was also tension in all areas of industry during the period as industrial leaders condemned the government's policy on welfare payments and openly demanded a more disciplined workforce. The trade unions, for their part, were determined to defend whatever advances had been achieved and were encouraged in this by the SPD. These developments are not indicated in the statistics.

SOURCES

2. POLITICAL STABILITY?

Source G: Reichstag election results (number of seats), 1924–31.

	May 1924	Dec 1924	1928
NSDAP	32	14	12
DNVP	95	103	73
DVP	45	51	45
Centre	65	69	62
DDP	28	32	25
SPD	100	131	153
KPD	62	45	54

Source H: from the Proclamation by President Hindenburg to the German people, 12 May 1925.

I have taken my new important office. True to my oath, I shall do everything in my power to serve the well-being of the German people, to protect the constitution and the laws, and to exercise justice for every man. In this solemn hour I ask the entire German people to work with me. My office and my efforts do not belong to any single class, nor to any stock or confession, nor to any party, but to all the German people strengthened in all its bones by a hard destiny.

Source I: Stresemann's speech to the Executive Committee of the DVP, 26 February 1928.

Let us not fool ourselves about this: we are in the midst of a parliamentary crisis that is already more than a crisis of conscience. The crisis has two roots: one the caricature that has become the parliamentary system in Germany, secondly the completely false position of parliament in relation to its responsibility to the nation.

Source J: from the recollections of Albert Krebs, *Gauleiter* of Hamburg.

Characteristic of this period was the steady disappearance of all leaders and subordinate leaders whose views and methods of struggle were still rooted in pre-war days. Their places were taken by the young men of what was known as the front generation of 25–35 years old.

Source K: from the Nazi newspaper, *The Munich Observer*, 31 May 1928, eleven days after the Reichstag election.

The election results from the rural areas in particular have proved that with a smaller expenditure of energy, money and time, better results can be achieved there than in the big cities.

Source L: from an article on Hitler by Gregor Strasser, 1927.

This is the great secret of our movement: an utter devotion to the idea of National Socialism, a glowing faith in the victorious strength of this doctrine of liberation and deliverance, is combined with a deep love of the person of our leader who is the shining hero of the new freedom fighters.

Questions

1. What were the names of the parties indicated by the initials DNVP, DVP and SPD? [3]
2. To what extent does the evidence of Source G show that there was political stability in the Weimar Republic between 1924 and 1929? [3]
*3. Compare the political message presented in Sources H and I. Using the attributions of the sources, and your own knowledge, explain the reason for the differences. [6]
4. Does the evidence of Source G conflict with the messages of Sources J, K and L? [6]

5. Using these sources and your own knowledge, how secure
    was democracy in Germany between 1925 and 1929? [7]

Worked answer

*3. The political messages of Sources H and I present a striking
contrast with each other. The tone of Source H is one of optimism,
whereas that of Source I of pessimism: Stresemann was all too conscious of being 'in the midst of a crisis'. Source H projects a positive
view of the political system, Hindenburg promising to 'do everything in
my power to serve the well-being of the German people'. Source I, on
the other hand, refers to 'the caricature that has become the parliamentary system in Germany'. Hindenburg projected confidence that
he could serve the nation without favour to 'any single class' or 'stock'
or 'confession' or 'party'. Stresemann's key message, however, was
the weakness of the parliamentary system and its 'false position' in
relation 'to its responsibility to the nation'.

These contrasts can be explained in terms of the occasions on
which the statements were made. A proclamation delivered after winning the presidency demanded a display of optimism and confidence:
anything less would imply that Hindenburg was incapable of the task
ahead. Stresemann had a different purpose. He was trying to pull
his party, the DVP, together as the linchpin of a faltering coalition. His
speech was intended for a small audience, the party's Executive
Committee, and, because it would not go to the nation at large, he
could afford to be frank: 'Let us not fool ourselves about this.' Bland
generalisations of the type used by Hindenburg would have been
useless in the circumstances.

There was also a contrast in the political experience of the two
statesmen. Hindenburg had up until that point no such experience and
was approaching an entirely new task. Stresemann, on the other hand,
had been struggling for years to manufacture parliamentary majorities
to keep coalitions together as well as preventing his own right-wing
bringing internal collapse to the DVP. The year 1928 was particularly
difficult and the 'crisis' referred to eventually resulted in a Reichstag
election. Despite the wording of the messages in the two sources,
Stresemann actually cared far more than Hindenburg for Weimar's
democratic system.

6

FOREIGN POLICY

BACKGROUND NARRATIVE

The foreign policy of the Weimar Republic was concerned almost entirely with coming to terms with the new Europe created by the Paris peace settlement. The initial priority was to try to soften the blow of the Treaty of Versailles. Wirth's administration (1921–22) carried out a policy of partial co-operation, or 'fulfilment' concerning the reparations terms, but this did not prevent the French from invading the Ruhr in January 1923. Wirth had more success in his attempt to establish contacts with Soviet Russia, with which Germany signed the Treaty of Rapallo in 1922. This provided for mutual diplomatic recognition and for industrial and commercial co-operation.

Improved relations between Germany and the western powers were largely the result of the efforts of Gustav Stresemann, Foreign Minister between 1923 and 1929. They started on an economic level with the signature of the Dawes Plan (1924) which extended the deadlines for the payment of reparations, a process taken further by the Young Plan of 1929. The first agreement concerning security, however, was drawn up at Locarno in 1925. The Treaty of Mutual Guarantee was intended to maintain the existing borders between Germany and France and those between Germany and Belgium. Britain and Italy were included as co-guarantors. Should any of the signatories threaten the specified border, the others would immediately request the permission of the Council of the League of Nations to take defensive action. This initiated the system of 'collective security'. France also wanted a similar undertaking to guarantee Germany's frontiers with Poland and Czechoslovakia. Stresemann refused to be drawn into this but he did prepare separate bilateral arbitration treaties with the two countries. He signified Germany's commitment to permanent peace by taking Germany into the League of Nations in 1926 (the year in which he was awarded the Nobel Peace Prize) and signing the Kellogg–Briand Pact (1928), whereby Germany and over 60 other countries agreed to 'renounce the use of war in their relations with each other'. Meanwhile, Stresemann had also taken relations with Russia a step further through the Treaty of Berlin, whereby each country agreed not to be drawn into any diplomatic or economic combination targeted at the other. By the time that Stresemann died in 1929, relations between Germany and the rest of Europe had improved considerably and the Allies were already pulling out, before schedule, the troops they had placed in the Rhineland under the terms of the Treaty of Versailles.

The last three years of the Weimar Republic saw a less conciliatory approach by the governments of Brüning, Papen and Schleicher. The main emphasis of their foreign policy was the end of reparations payments which, they argued, Germany could no longer pay, devastated as she was by the Depression which hit her in 1929. President Hoover allowed a moratorium on payments in 1930 and this was extended at the Lausanne Conference (1932) to virtual cancellation. Thus the most contentious component of the Treaty of Versailles had been removed.

But, for the time being at least, the military and territorial provisions remained in force. The governments of the Weimar Republic had little option but to accept these. The army's leadership, however, had different ideas. Von Seeckt and Stülpnagel had a programme which would eventually reverse the Treaty of Versailles and full use was made of the improved relations with Russia to carry out secret rearmament – the extent of which not even the government was fully aware.

ANALYSIS (1): WHAT WERE THE AIMS AND METHODS OF THE FOREIGN POLICY OF THE WEIMAR REPUBLIC?

The underlying aim of all who had anything to do with foreign policy in the Weimar Republic was to secure a revision of the peace settlement. The terms were deeply unpopular. All Germans were outraged by the War Guilt Clause and felt it essential to remove the yoke of reparations payments. Most were deeply unhappy about the boundary changes which left their fellow-countrymen as minority communities in other states. Many were deeply resentful of the military restrictions which appeared to deprive Germany of the right to self-defence. A substantial minority took revisionism even further and argued the case for Anschluss with Austria. There was therefore unanimity that the Treaty needed to be changed – but not over which areas should be given priority and how the changes were to be achieved. Two strands gradually emerged in Germany's revisionist policy. One might be referred to as the 'political' approach. This was based on the official government policy of Chancellors like Wirth, or Foreign Ministers like Stresemann, and emphasised the use of diplomacy to achieve realistic targets over a long time-scale. This contrasted with the 'military' approach. Officers of the Reichswehr, especially von Stülpnagel and von Seeckt, were more impatient to evade the disarmament clause and to revise Germany's boundaries in eastern Europe. After 1931 the two strands began to converge, preparing the way for Hitler's policies.

The 'political' or 'official' approach to foreign policy was of necessity pragmatic. The priority had to be the revision of the Treaty of Versailles according to Germany's most pressing needs. The most urgent priority from 1921 was to remove the intolerable burden of reparations – using whatever method was to hand. This explains Wirth's policy of 'fulfilment' between 1921 and 1922, which aimed at co-operation with the Allies to persuade them that the terms of the Treaty of Versailles were unduly harsh and therefore needed to be modified. Wirth also envisaged reconciliation with the other powers in Europe, but, disillusioned with the way in which the western countries sought to enforce the full rigour of reparations, he sought his first *rapprochement* with Russia. The result was the Rapallo Treaty of 1922, which was a pragmatic agreement between the two pariahs of Europe. It was, however, an arrangement born of desperation and it did nothing to help Wirth's search for reconciliation with the West; if anything, it confirmed French suspicions that Germany was trying to evade reparations altogether and it precipitated the invasion of the Ruhr in 1923. Clearly government policy had to become more systematic – and, if necessary, more devious.

This combination was provided by Stresemann, Foreign Minister between 1923 and 1929. He incorporated an element of Wirth's 'fulfilment' into a policy which was, however, more complex in its overall conception. He has, however, been the subject of considerable debate among historians, who range from admirers of his idealism to critics of his ruthlessness. Two perceptions of Stresemann are especially radical. One is that he was an early European integrationist, a theme developed by German historians during the 1950s. In retrospect this view seems to have been motivated by Germany's search for rehabilitation and a new role after the Second World War rather than as a genuine appreciation of what Stresemann was actually trying to do. At the other extreme, Stresemann was once seen as a covert nationalist, seeking to lull Europe into a false sense of security while preparing Germany for an active policy of revisionism. The evidence for this was based on his letter to the Crown Prince in 1925, in which he declared his intentions to include the 'protection of Germans abroad' together with 'the readjustment of our eastern frontiers; the recovery of Danzig, the Polish corridor, and a correction of the frontier in Upper Silesia'. (1) According to some historians Stresemann remained in essence what he had been throughout the First World War, an ardent advocate of power politics and conquest. Ruge, for example, maintains that 'Stresemann's long-term policy was one of preparing for warlike expansion' and that he 'worked towards a war, but always kept in view that armed force as a political instrument was, under certain conditions, not calculated to serve the interests of the classes he represented'. (2) But this is a Marxist view and is therefore locked into a scenario of class interest: this is especially apparent in the second half of the quotation. It also discounts the possibility that Stresemann may have discarded his more nationalistic preferences and adapted to the changed circumstances of post-Versailles Europe.

It is possible to present an alternative view of Stresemann which makes more sense of his diplomatic skills. In outline, he made commitments where there was little chance of doing anything else and tried to create opportunities where there was room for manoeuvre: he tied down Germany in the West in order to free her up in the East. Such a strategy was more complex than that pursued by Wirth but was well within the acumen of Stresemann who, as a tough pragmatist, recognised the need to adapt to changing times and circumstances while creating, where possible, new opportunities for the future.

The West was the source of Germany's main difficulties and where the most immediate resolutions were needed. To secure these, Stresemann realised, Germany would have to make concessions. His main aim was to secure direct access to the economic strength and assistance of the United States. This would serve to enlist American help in reducing Allied suspicion and it would improve Germany's own position. Hence in his words 'A revision of the Versailles Treaty will not be achieved by the force of arms, but by the forces of the world-economic community of interests of the nations.' (3) Closely linked to this was the need to solve the reparations problem. He was prepared to commit Germany to the Dawes Plan (1924) and to paying the full amount of reparations, albeit over an extended period, because in return Germany would receive American investments. In other words, he agreed to give up the option (which did not really exist) of resisting reparations in exchange for a major material concession. The same principle influenced his agreement to the Locarno Pact (1925). He saw it as a major priority to remove the French threat from Germany but was realistic enough to see that he would have to remove the threat which Germany appeared to pose for France. The solution was collective security and a guarantee of Germany's borders with France and Belgium. Stresemann saw that Germany could not possibly regain her losses from Versailles by the threat of military action, since her military strength no longer existed. Hence he was agreeing to the removal of an option which Germany did not have. In exchange, he prevented the French from making use of an option which they *did* have. By locking Germany into the commitment of collective security in the West, Stresemann aimed to deny France any possible reason – or excuse – to take action against Germany in the future. Never again would the French be able to invade the Ruhr, as they had done in 1923.

Commitments in the West would be compensated by freeing up the situation in the East. Here Stresemann aimed to create diplomatic options for the future. The most effective way of doing this was by undermining the French security system there. This would work in two ways: it would reduce the perceived need of France to have eastern allies, and it would create uncertainty among the latter about France's real intentions. In order to achieve flexibility in the East, however, Stresemann refused to extend the general principle of collective security to Poland and Czechoslovakia. Instead of another Treaty of Mutual Guarantee, underpinned by France, Britain and Italy, Stresemann agreed in 1925 only to bilateral Arbitration Treaties involving Germany, Poland and Czechoslovakia. He also continued to develop the link with Russia, started in 1922 by Wirth. The Treaty of Berlin (1926) amounted to a military non-aggression pact. This has been seen by Gatzke and others as an indication that Stresemann was considering long-term military action in eastern Europe, at Poland's expense. This is not necessarily true. It makes more sense to see the connection with the Soviet Union as a further means of reducing French influence in eastern Europe. This could well yield substantial diplomatic concessions in the future; Stresemann was prepared to wait for his revisionist hopes to be realised.

All of Stresemann's diplomacy, whether agreeing to commitments in the West or freeing up room for manoeuvre in the East, involved expressions of peace, reconciliation and goodwill. Hence he worked hard to secure Germany's admission to the League of Nations in 1926 and was content to commit Germany to the Kellogg Briand Pact of 1928. He also projected Germany as 'the bridge which would bring East and West together in the development of Europe'. Again, these have been seen as an insincere attempt to divert attention from darker policies being harboured below the surface. But they are more likely to have been diplomatic gestures intended to increase the credibility of a statesman who was prepared to balance short-term concessions with the hope of long-term gain. Stresemann was thinking in terms of revisionism through diplomacy, not through war.

All this was in contrast with the 'military' approach to foreign policy. There were strong influences within the Reichswehr for the systematic rearmament of Germany and for preparations to complete the unfinished business of the First World War. Whereas Stresemann and the diplomats had altered their nationalist views as a result of the changed circumstances of 1919, the military commanders did not. They therefore combined revisionism with the achievement of earlier objectives. In 1915, for example, Admiral von Tirpitz stated that many circles in the army were saying that 'although Germany should have conducted power politics, it should have been a continental policy'. (4) General Groener reinforced this when he said in 1919: 'we have unconsciously aimed at world domination before we had secured our continental position.' (5) The corollary to this was that German supremacy should be sought in strictly military terms in the future. The repudiation of the Treaty of Versailles should be the first step. Typical of this approach was the list provided by Colonel von Stuelpnagel in 1926. This included the 'liberation of the Rhineland and Saar area', the return of German lands in Poland, the 'Anschluss of German Austria' and 'the abolition of the Demilitarised Zone'. (6) General von Seeckt had similar views and, as early as 1922, was speaking of the dismantling of Poland. In his Memorandum of 11 September 1922 he argued that Poland's existence was 'intolerable, incompatible with the survival of Germany' and that 'it must disappear'. This would have a direct impact on France, for 'with Poland falls one of the strongest pillars of the Treaty of Versailles, the preponderance of France'. Hence the Reichswehr was determined to exploit to the full any opportunity to revise or undermine the Treaty of Versailles. To the diplomacy of the politicians would therefore be added certain military preparations. Hence von Seeckt pursued a policy of secret rearmament by using the link established with Russia at Rapallo. This would involve 'a direct strengthening of ourselves, by helping to create in Russia an armaments industry which in case of need will serve us'. (7) Germany also used her special relationship with Russia as a means of evading the rearmament restrictions imposed by the Treaty of Versailles. The Reichswehr derived a great deal from secret training and manoeuvres on Russian soil. Von Seeckt was, however, wary of trusting the politicians: he argued that 'the participation and even the official knowledge of the German government must be entirely excluded. The details of the negotiations must remain in the hands of the military authorities.' (8) It is unlikely that Stresemann was entirely ignorant of what was happening here. It may even be that he saw certain advantages in secret rearmament. But, rather than considering diplomacy as a preparation for war, he saw any military strengthening going on below the surface as a means ultimately of strengthening his diplomacy.

Until 1929 there was therefore a significant contrast between the political and military objectives of foreign policy. After the death of Stresemann, however, the two main elements began to come together. This coincided from 1931 with the Republic's lurch to the right and the army's growing influence in politics. The administrations of Brüning, von Papen and von Schleicher lost the diplomatic subtlety shown by Stresemann and instead began to follow the more obvious military line of exploiting any advantages gained. This was reflected to some extent by a change in personnel. One of the key officials behind Stresemann's policies, von Schubert, was replaced in 1930 by von Bülow. He differed profoundly from Stresemann in being more impatient over the settlement of the reparations issue and he encouraged Brüning to take a more forceful line, a process continued by the Papen government. The cancellation of remaining reparations by the Lausanne Conference (1932) was attributed to this pressure and, from this time onwards, diplomatic and military objectives converged. It is hardly surprising that when Hitler came to power he found a large degree of willingness within Germany to support his revision of the military clauses of the Treaty of Versailles. In the final analysis, however, the continuity was with the ideas of von Seeckt, not with those of Stresemann.

Questions

1. Who had the more realistic view of what was needed in German foreign policy between 1920 and 1932: the politicians or the military commanders?
2. How sincere was Stresemann in his diplomacy with other countries between 1923 and 1929?

ANALYSIS (2): HOW SUCCESSFUL WAS THE FOREIGN POLICY OF GUSTAV STRESEMANN?

Success and failure are often seen as absolute terms. In fact, they are relative. It is possible to give quite different answers depending on the perspective adopted.

Take failure. It could be argued, from the longer term perspective, that Stresemann achieved very little. By 1929 he was himself disappointed by how much of the Treaty of Versailles remained intact. All he had managed to do was to secure the rescheduling of the reparations payments by the Dawes Plan (1924) and the early withdrawal of Allied troops from the Rhineland in 1929. Even this was slower than Stresemann had hoped, as France firmly resisted early proposals for a general evacuation. A German delegation to the League of Nations in 1928 requested the complete withdrawal from the Rhineland without guarantees but the French and British continued to insist on guarantees for reparations payments. This meant that any agreement on withdrawal had to be linked to the Young Plan (1929) which made Germany liable to continue payments until the 1980s. Having to agree to this was in part a humiliation for Stresemann and he was fiercely criticised by the combined forces of the right. Indeed, the close collaboration over this between the DNVP and the Nazis did much to make Hitler appear more respectable to the German electorate.

Nor did Stresemann succeed in securing a revision of any of the other terms of the Treaty of Versailles. No frontier adjustments had even been discussed and the possibility of restoring any German minorities to the Fatherland was as far off as ever. The military clauses remained intact, the Rhineland was still demilitarised, the army continued to be held to 100,000, and the absolute prohibition on any air force remained intact. Germany had no means of defending herself against any future allied invasion and her military and naval capacity was still well below that of Britain and France, and because of the artificial constraints of Versailles, lower than those of Italy, Poland and Russia. Any real developments occurred after Stresemann's period in office, largely as a result of the more forceful diplomacy and demands of Brüning and then Hitler. This almost makes it appear that the 'military' strategy of von Seeckt and others was right after all: covert rearmament was the only approach to revisionism which stood a remote chance of working. In any case, Stresemann's policy of moderate diplomacy collapsed in two stages after 1929 – first under the impact of the Depression and then as a result of the policies pursued by Hitler.

There is, however, an alternative perspective. The longer term disintegration of a system does not necessarily prove that it was a failure. Most historians consider that Stresemann's diplomacy achieved a great deal during his lifetime: Kolb, for one, says, 'it must be acknowledged that his six years in office were astonishingly successful'. (9) This would certainly stand the test of a direct comparison between the situations of 1923 and 1929. When Stresemann became Chancellor, and then Foreign Minister, Germany was isolated and vulnerable in the West. She could not fulfil her obligations over reparations; nor could she convince the Allies that she lacked the means to do so. The government could only stand by and suffer the indignity of a French invasion – which had not even happened during the First World War. There was in all this no moderating influence from the United States, which had withdrawn into isolation. It must have seemed that Germany was even worse off in 1923 than she had been in 1919. It is true that she had formed, at Rapallo in 1922, an agreement with Russia. But this was more than counterbalanced by the close relations developed by France with Poland, which was itself perceived as a major military threat: Polish troops had, after all, defeated the Red army in the Russo–Polish War of 1921–22. The situation in eastern Europe was therefore only marginally better than than in the West. Never before had Germany been so hemmed in by enemies and so helpless in her response.

By the time of Stresemann's death the situation had been transformed in several ways. First, the Dawes Plan (1924) had brought in the United States to underpin the German economy through a series of substantial loans. All Germany had to do in return was to agree to make reparations payments in instalments, something she was in no position to refuse. As it turned out, Germany actually received more from the new arrangement than she paid out. Second, the Locarno Pact (1925) ensured that France would never again invade German territory; all that Germany gave up in return was the option of attacking France, which she was in no position to do. Third, the situation in eastern Europe had become more flexible, with the French system of security looking increasingly vulnerable and offset by the Treaty of Berlin (1926), a virtual non-aggression pact between Germany and Russia. Finally, Germany's reputation had been immeasurably enhanced by her entry into the League of Nations in 1926 and her signing of the Kellogg Briand Pact (1928). Stresemann received personal credit and acknowledgement when he was awarded the Nobel Peace Prize in 1926.

It is true that Stresemann's achievements were partly offset by the impact of the Depression after 1929 and that the decline of his moderating influence is often seen as long-term failure. There is, however, a case for saying that successes in Germany's foreign policy in the 1930s would have been impossible without his diplomacy. It is difficult to see how the Allies would have agreed so readily to the cancellation of the reparations in 1932 unless they had been fundamentally impressed by Germany's rehabilitation and her new importance as part of the international economic order. Similarly, Britain and France were a great deal more tolerant during the 1930s of Hitler's blows against the Treaty of Versailles than they ever would have been in the 1920s. In part, this was due to belated recognition that the Treaty had been too harsh, a conclusion made possible by the moderation shown by German policy in the meantime. It is ironic that the real beneficiary of this perception was not the Weimar Republic of Stresemann but the Third Reich. Much of what was eventually achieved by Hitler was made possible by Stresemann but would not have been approved by him.

Questions

1. Is there a stronger case for Stresemann's success than for his failure in foreign policy?
2. 'Stresemann's foreign policy succeeded in the short term but not in the long term.' Do you agree?

SOURCES

1. THE POLICIES OF STRESEMANN

Source A: from a confidential letter to the ex-Crown Prince from Stresemann, 7 September 1925.

In my opinion there are three great tasks that confront German foreign policy in the more immediate future.

In the first place the solution of the Reparations question in a sense tolerable for Germany . . .

Secondly, the protection of Germans abroad, those 10 to 12 million of our kindred who now live under a foreign yoke in foreign lands.

The third great task is the readjustment of our eastern frontiers; the recovery of Danzig, the Polish corridor, and a correction of the frontier in Upper Silesia.

In the background stands the union with German Austria, although I am quite clear that this not merely brings no advantages to Germany, but seriously complicates the problem of the German Reich . . .

The Locarno Pact rules out the possibility of any military conflict with France for the recovery of Alsace-Lorraine . . .

The question of a choice between east and west does not arise as the result of our joining the League. Such a choice can only be made when backed by military force. That, alas, we do not possess . . .

Source B: from a speech by Stresemann defending the Locarno Pact, 15 December 1925.

I see the importance in another connection of this security for peace between ourselves and France. It is true that these are all matters that lie in the future; a nation must not adopt the attitude of a child that writes a list of its wants on Christmas Eve, which contains everything that the child will need for the next fifteen years. The parents would not be in a position to give it all this. In foreign politics I often have the feeling that I am being confronted with such a list, and that it is forgotten that history advances merely step by step.

Source C: from Stresemann's speech to the League of Nations, two days after Germany's accession, 10 September 1926.

. . . the German Government may well speak for the great majority of the German race when it declares that it will wholeheartedly devote itself to the duties devolving upon the League of Nations . . .

Germany's relations to the League are not, however, confined exclusively to the possibilities of co-operation in general aims and issues. In many respects the

League is the heir and executor of the Treaties of 1919. Out of these Treaties there have arisen in the past, I may say frankly, many differences between the League and Germany. I hope that our co-operation within the League will make it easier in future to discuss these questions. In this respect mutual confidence will, from a political point of view, be found a greater creative force than anything else.

Questions

1. Who was Stresemann? (Source A) [2]
   Who were the powers signing the Locarno Pact (Source B)? [2]
2. What are the similarities between the content of Sources A, B and C? [4]
3. What are the differences between the content of Sources A, B and C? [4]
*4. Do Sources A, B and C show that Stresemann was pursuing a 'two-faced policy' towards Europe? [6]
5. Using these sources, and your own knowledge, do you agree that Stresemann's reputation was likely to have been greater outside than inside Germany? [7]

Worked answer

*4. [It is important to identify the examples of apparent inconsistency but, at the same time, to avoid too obvious a conclusion.]

There certainly appears to be some support for the view that Stresemann was 'two-faced'. He seemed to pursue a strongly revisionist line in Source A, aiming at 'the readjustment of our eastern frontiers' and the recovery of Danzig and the Polish corridor. In Source B, by contrast, he warned against the childish listing of territorial demands which could only undermine the 'mutual confidence' and 'co-operation' he sought in Source C. Some historians have inferred from such evidence that Stresemann did indeed have a hidden agenda as well as an open one for diplomacy. This might be backed by the difference in the attributions between A on the one hand and B and C on the other.

An alternative view is that Stresemann had consistent views in all three sources. In Source A he could afford to be less guarded in his references since he was writing in confidence; even here, however, he drew the line at something as radical as a 'union with German Austria'. Source B carried a more cautiously worded message that changes could not be accomplished immediately, since 'history advances merely step by step'. Nevertheless, as he remarked in Source C, the League could expect to be faced with unfinished business since the League was 'the heir and executor of the Treaties of 1919'. Instead of being two-faced, therefore, Stresemann was merely adapting his language to the occasion but saying essentially the same thing on each.

SOURCES

2. GERMANY AND RUSSIA 1922–26

Source D: from the Rapallo Pact between Germany and Russia, 16 April 1922.

ARTICLE 1. Both governments agree that the differences between Germany and Russia during the time of war have been resolved on the following matters:

a. The German Reich and the Russian Soviet Republic mutually renunciate compensation for war costs as well as compensation for war damages . . .

ARTICLE 3. Diplomatic and consular relations between the German Reich and the Soviet government shall be resumed immediately . . .

ARTICLE 4. Both governments further are agreed that the general legal rights of nationals of one country in the other are re-established, and that regulations be made for a revival of trade and industrial relations . . .

ARTICLE 5. Both governments shall regard the industrial needs of their countries in a mutually favourable spirit.

Source E: from a Memorandum by General von Seeckt, 11 September 1922.

Poland's existence is intolerable, incompatible with the survival of Germany. It must disappear, and will disappear through its own internal weakness and through Russia – with our assistance. For Russia Poland is even more intolerable than for us; no Russian can allow Poland to exist. With Poland falls one of the strongest pillars of the Treaty of Versailles, the preponderance of France . . . The re-establishment of the broad common frontier between Russia and Germany is the precondition for the regaining of strength of both countries . . .

We aim at two things: first, a strengthening of Russia in the economic and political, thus also in the military field, and so indirectly a strengthening of ourselves, by strengthening a possible ally of the future; we further desire, at first cautiously and experimentally, a direct strengthening of ourselves, by helping to create in Russia an armaments industry which in case of need will serve us . . .

In all these enterprises, which to a large extent are only beginning, the participation and even the official knowledge of the German government must be entirely excluded. The details of the negotiations must remain in the hands of the military authorities.

Source F: from the Russo–German Treaty, 24 April 1926.

ARTICLE 1. The Treaty of Rapallo remains the basis of relations between Germany and the Union of Soviet Socialist Republics . . .

ARTICLE 2. If one of the contracting parties, despite its peaceful attitude, should be attacked by a third power or by several third powers, the other contracting party shall observe neutrality during the period of conflict.

ARTICLE 3. If, in the event of a conflict of the nature foreshadowed in Article 2, occurring at a time when either of the two contracting parties is not involved in an armed conflict, a coalition should be formed by third powers with a view to imposing an economic and financial boycott on one of the two contracting parties, the other contracting party will not participate in such a coalition.

Source G: from Hitler's *Mein Kampf*.

Thus we National Socialists consciously put an end to the foreign policy of the prewar period. We begin again where things ended six centuries ago. We put a stop to the eternal drive of the Teuton towards Europe's South and West, and cast our eyes to the land of the East . . . But if we speak of new soil and territory in Europe today, we can think primarily only of Russia and of the subject states bordering it . . .

Questions

1. Who was General von Seeckt (Source E)? [1]
    What alternative name is sometimes given to the Russo–German Treaty (Source F)? [1]
2. Why did von Seeckt consider it necessary that 'the official knowledge of the German government must be entirely excluded' (Source E)? [4]

3. To what extent was Source D modified by Source F? Why did the German government consider this to be necessary? [6]

*4. How did Hitler's conception of Germany's relation with Russia (Source G) differ from that of von Seeckt (Source E)? How would you explain this difference? [6]

5. Using the sources, and your own knowledge, would you agree that the German government and the German army were pursuing different aims in their relations with Russia during the 1920s? [7]

Worked answer

*4. [The answer to the first part of the question is largely in the sources. The answer to the second part requires additional information.]

The conceptions of both von Seeckt and Hitler were radical, envisaging major changes to the map of Europe. The way in which these would be accomplished, however, were markedly different. Von Seeckt's target was Poland, whose very existence was 'intolerable, incompatible with the survival of Germany'; Russia, by contrast, was 'a possible ally of the future'. Hitler drew no distinction between 'Russia and of the subject states bordering it'. Hence von Seeckt envisaged close co-operation with Russia in the dismantling of Poland, whereas Hitler proposed the same fate for both.

The reason for this difference was a contrasting vision of German needs. For von Seeckt the priority was to dismantle the Versailles settlement, of which 'one of the strongest pillars' was France. The collapse of Poland in the East would undermine France in the West. Von Seeckt was therefore advocating a radical form of revisionism in which Russia, as a diplomatic outcast in Europe, had a useful role to play. Hitler's aims were more fundamental, encompassing 'new soil and territory', or Lebensraum at the expense of the whole of eastern Europe. Russia had nothing to offer Germany, being the centre of Bolshevism and international Jewry. Hitler's ideology therefore contrasted with von Seeckt's pragmatism.

7

CRISIS AND COLLAPSE, 1929–33

BACKGROUND NARRATIVE

If there was a period of relative stability between 1924 and 1929, it was soon ended by economic and political developments between 1929 and 1933.

The Wall Street Crash was the catalyst for economic crisis as the short-term loans and investments, poured into Germany by the United States after 1924, were suddenly recalled. This resulted in a massive cutback in industrial production which, in turn, led to increased unemployment levels. The banking system was seriously affected by the collapse of Kredit Anstaldt in Vienna in 1931. Germany was clearly in no state to be able to continue reparations payments, which were cancelled at Lausanne in 1932.

Meanwhile, the Republic was sliding from democracy into authoritarianism. The grand coalition, comprising the SPD, DDP, Centre Party and DVP, broke up in 1930, ostensibly in a dispute over the continuation of unemployment benefits. Müller resigned the Chancellorship, taking the SPD with him. His successor, Brüning, was unable to command a majority in the Reichstag and resorted increasingly to the use of Article 48 of the Constitution: President Hindenburg was happy to allow him to govern by emergency decree. This process was accelerated under Brüning's two successors as Chancellor in 1932: first Papen, then Schleicher. The Reichstag attempted to restrict the President's use of Article 48 but was dissolved twice in 1932. The two elections which followed considerably increased the strength of anti-Republican forces, the Nazis becoming for the first time the largest party in the Reichstag.

The growth of the right in Germany is the really distinctive feature of the period 1929–33. This manifested itself in two ways. The first was the consolidation of the conservative or reactionary right, which found security in the use of presidential powers and aimed quite deliberately at undermining the parliamentary process of which it had long disapproved. The second was the rapid growth of the radical or revolutionary right. Hitler's popular support rose rapidly in the elections of 1930 and 1932, encouraging him to make a bid for the presidency in 1932. When he was defeated by Hindenburg, who was re-elected by a convincing margin, Hitler aimed instead at the Chancellorship. He became involved in an intrigue with Papen against the latter's personal rival, Schleicher, and Hindenburg was persuaded to appoint Hitler Chancellor on 30 January 1933. Within two days, Hitler sought an election. In March 1933, the Nazis improved their position in the Reichstag. With the support of the Centre Party, they proceeded to pass the Enabling Act. This, in effect, institutionalised the use of Article 48, allowing the Chancellor to rule by decree and bypass the Reichstag. Under its provisions, the new regime banned all parties apart from the NSDAP, thereby destroying the last vestiges of democracy and converting the authoritarian dictatorship of Hindenburg into a totalitarian one under Hitler.

ANALYSIS (1): WHY DID WEIMAR DEMOCRACY COLLAPSE AFTER 1929?

The collapse of Weimar democracy is often ascribed to one of two reasons. First, the Republic was foredoomed because of its origins and its inherent flaws. Or, second, it was killed off, during the period in which it was actually thriving, by an external calamity over which it could have had no control. These interpretations are mutually exclusive but they share the same defect. They are both monocausal. Instead, we should expect a more complex explanation of the Republic's collapse. For example, a multiplicity of factors were involved, which upset the Republic's equilibrium and made it vulnerable to sudden shock. Although the Depression was vitally important, Germany was alone among the major powers to have been affected by it to the point of actual constitutional change. Italy was already a dictatorship, while Britain and France both survived the impact of the Depression by adapting their political systems to deal with its effects. This means that Germany must have had a set of circumstances to make it uniquely susceptible. The Depression did not start the process of decline; it acted as a turning point. It was not an initiator; it was a catalyst or accelerator.

The long-term factors which upset the political and economic equilibrium within Germany had been building up for some time and have already been examined separately. They came together as follows.

The political structure of the Weimar Republic was inherently vulnerable. This was partly because of the incomplete nature of its changeover from the Second Reich and the survival of conservative forces which were its constant enemy: these were most apparent in the army and in the DNVP. Although the Constitution created what was in many ways an advanced democracy, the existence of Article 48 was always potential for the translation of this conservatism into dictatorship. This was not immediately apparent, since the Republic was initially in moderate hands and Ebert used Article 48 sparingly. However, during the period 1924–29 the constant strain of coalition governments began to show in growing disillusionment with party politics, even by those most directly involved. At the same time, the right gained latent strength through the election of President Hindenburg in 1925 and the growing unity of the right. Hence it could be argued that there was already considerable potential for political collapse even before the Depression occurred.

The economy also played a vital role. The maxim that political crisis is accelerated by economic crisis holds true. The strains of the Depression in 1930 and 1931 proved too great for Germany's political system to bear, yet this was not some sudden extraneous blow to a thriving system. The economic structure of the Republic had several fundamental flaws which made it highly vulnerable to external pressures. One was the establishment of a network of dependence on American loans, a legacy of the Dawes Plan which had been intended to make the payment of reparations more realistic. Another was the use of short-term investments to finance long-term projects and to avoid increasing taxation. A third was the development of industrial production without a corresponding expansion of consumerism within Germany and trade outside. Sooner or later it would become evident that Germany was living beyond her means. How would the political system respond to the pressures which this would create?

This long-term vulnerability was converted into collapse by the catalyst of the Depression. As between 1920 and 1923, the Republic faced a crisis – which, this time, it did not survive. How, precisely, did the Depression impact upon the economic structure and exacerbate the political crisis? The main problem was the recall of short-term loans which had unwisely been committed to long-term projects. This immediately weakened the industrial and welfare infrastructure which meant that more people were made unemployed in Germany than in other major European economies hit by the Depression. The statistics are startling. The national income in 1932 was 39% less than it had been in 1929, while unemployment rose steadily from 1.3 million in 1929 to 3 million in 1930, 4.3 million in 1931, 5.1 million in 1932, and 6 million in 1933. The social and psychological effects of this were devastating. All social classes were affected, including the middle classes, who escaped relatively unscathed in Britain. The potential for discontent was considerable, enabling the enemies of the Republic to conduct a propaganda campaign against it. This, according to Kolb, showed just 'how weak were the foundations of Weimar democracy, in terms of the solidity of its institutions or the loyalty of influential social and political groups and large sections of the population.' (1) The ramifications of this were serious. Germany suffered disaster because its political system was not constructed to deal with the Depression. There is also a strong suspicion that opponents of the political system used the Depression as an excuse for changing that system. The collapse of democracy therefore involves a number of sub-questions.

First, when did the slide to dictatorship start? There is some disagreement about this among historians. According to Conze, the switch to presidential dictatorship was the inevitable result of the 'crisis of the party-political state'. (2) Meinecke takes a more immediate view, relating the onset of dictatorship to the dismissal of Brüning: otherwise 'it could very well have been able to survive the difficult economic and spiritual crisis and to avert the ruinous experiment of the Third Reich'. (3) Kolb, too, sees the appointment of Brüning as 'a far reaching and dangerous transformation of the system of government'. (4) But Brüning was trying to find an alternative to party politics which had clearly failed: in this respect he was also trying to avoid permanent dictatorship. Bracher is not so sure about the latter point, arguing that historians should avoid taking 'a conservative and all too benevolent view of the presidential regime'. (5) Hamburger agrees with Bracher: he maintains that Brüning was attempting from 1930 'to restore a constitutional order of the Bismarckian type by misusing the system of emergency decrees'. (6) This seems to receive some backing from the Memoirs of Brüning, published in 1970, which show a desire to move towards an anti-Republican position. It does certainly seem clear that Brüning was aware of the plans being made to undermine the Republic.

How was the movement to dictatorship accomplished? The general process involved a combination of planning and improvisation, of control over events and being controlled by events. An overall generalisation might be that the destruction of democracy was planned, but Hitler's appointment was the result of unforeseen events. We can also see a trend in the relations between the President and the Chancellor on the one hand and the Reichstag on the other. At first the administration made emergency decrees under Article 48 the main instrument of dictatorship. When these were eventually challenged by the Reichstag, it resorted to dissolutions and Reichstag elections. Since, however, these could not be repeated indefinitely, the next stage was political intrigue which became more and more unpredictable in its effects. It is the last of these three stages which ultimately brought Hitler to power.

The first stage involved the increased use of Article 48 as an alternative to submitting all legislation to the Reichstag. This was the result of a deliberate campaign, pursued by Hindenburg, the presidential entourage and the army, to undermine the Weimar Republic. Brüning also became involved, before he became Chancellor – and before the onset of the Depression. He was approached early in 1929 for his views on the formation of a 'presidential' cabinet in place of the administration of Müller, the SPD leader. The President, it seems, had already decided to form an 'anti-parliamentarian' and 'anti-Marxist' cabinet which would not include the SPD. Brüning went along with this and formed a cabinet without the SPD on 30 March 1930, reasonably secure in the knowledge that he had regular access to Article 48. The latter proved sufficient for a while. However, the Reichstag sought a way round this by voting for the abrogation of Article 48, refusing, for example, to accept Brüning's finance bill in July. From this point onwards, the President resorted to dissolving the Reichstag whenever it chose to exercise this power. The first occasion was in 1930. The election which followed produced a swing to the right and an apparent strengthening of Brüning's position and again he made full use of Article 48. For over a year the Reichstag was unable to secure a majority to cancel the President's right to issue decrees. This was largely because the opposition had to do without the SPD, which was playing a pragmatic game: the SPD hoped to keep afloat their coalition with the Centre Party in the state government of Prussia as a quid pro quo for not bringing Brüning down in central government, but the situation had changed by 1932. Brüning was forced to resign over a dispute concerning the future of unprofitable estates in eastern Germany. His successor, Papen, dismissed the government of Prussia and assumed direct control over it himself. From this point onwards, the SPD played a key part in the Reichstag's attack on Article 48, with the result that the President had to call two further elections: one in July, the other in November. By the end of 1932 Hindenburg was confronted by a real dilemma. He could not keep on dissolving the Reichstag for new elections; nor could he constitutionally do without the Reichstag altogether since Article 25 of the Constitution obliged him to call an election within 60 days. The onslaught on democracy therefore became more devious, involving plot and subterfuge rather than direct use of the constitution.

Hence dissolution was replaced by intrigue. To the distortion of the Constitution, right-wing dictatorship now added sabotage. Schleicher, who had once courted the support of Hitler, began to distrust him and, on replacing Papen as Chancellor in December 1932, sought to detach Strasser from the NSDAP to join his new administration. Furious, Hitler turned to Papen, who was aggrieved at the peremptory way in which Schleicher had taken his post. Secretly they undermined Schleicher's position and when the latter asked for a dissolution in January 1923, they put pressure on Hindenburg to refuse. Instead, they presented a scheme whereby Hitler would be appointed Chancellor, although of a coalition cabinet, of which Papen would be Vice-Chancellor. It seems never to have occurred to Hindenburg that he might actually take the initiative in promoting a more broadly based coalition. He was fully in accord with the aim of the right to avoid any possibility of a return to parliamentary government.

But why did the slide to authoritarian dictatorship lead to the appointment of Hitler and the risk of something more radical than either Papen or Hindenburg had in mind? There seems to be a contradiction here. At the very time that the Reichstag was being deliberately undermined, the NSDAP were increasing their representation within it. Might not the appointment of Hitler therefore be a step backwards into democracy and party politics? To be followed by a leap into the unknown? None of the politicians or theorists of the conservative right saw Nazism as a danger; instead they all envisaged it as an elemental power which could be harnessed and controlled. Radicalism, in other words, would be the force with which conservatism would destroy democracy. Instead of parliamentary politics, there would be a broad front of right-wing nationalist politicians in association with the army and industrialists. The NSDAP would have no option but to join this if it were to escape the trap of parliamentary politics. There was one other indication that Nazism would be likely to change its identity. In the second election of 1932 the NSDAP experienced a decline in the number of seats from 230 to 196, while the DNVP increased from 37 to 52. Nazism had, it seemed, peaked as a parliamentary party – another reason for assuming that it would be a willing partner in the new identity of the broad right. In addition, Hitler had lost his bid in 1932 to oust Hindenburg as President. A party in decline, with a leader who had recently suffered a resounding personal defeat, provided more of an opportunity than a threat. To ensure that this remained the case, Hitler was appointed subject to the constraints of having only three Nazis in his cabinet and Papen's Vice-Chancellorship. Within two months, Papen argued, 'we will have pushed Hitler so far into a corner that he'll squeak'. (7) The whole strategy of the conservative right was based upon a misconception of proportions unequalled in modern history.

How, in the meantime, had Hitler been able to increase his electoral support to the point of attracting the interest of the reactionary right and enticing them into making such a blunder? The Depression undoubtedly catapulted the Nazis into the position of Germany's second largest party as a result of the 1930 election. This was due partly to the conversion of existing voters and partly to their capture of the new vote (there were 4 million extra votes in 1930 compared with 1928). Existing support was diverted mainly from the DNVP, DVP and DDP, underlining that the defection was at least partly a middle-class phenomenon; this view has been advanced by historians such as Bullock, Bracher, Knauerhase and Kornhauser. Other historians see new support as the crucial factor in Nazi success. This came from a variety of classes and cannot be confined to the defection of the middle classes. The SPD also suffered from defections to the Nazis, indicating that radicalised members of the working class were as likely to swing to the far right as they were to the Communist left. The Nazis also gained a considerable increase in support from the industrial and business communities, in addition to a few prominent individuals such as Thyssen who had been supporting the Nazis for some time. They were, in the last analysis, the only party able to project an appeal to all social classes within Germany and to all sectors of the population. It is small wonder, therefore, that the conservative right valued the NSDAP as a channel for the widespread transmission of authoritarian values.

Overall, it is important to avoid monocausal assumptions. The collapse of the Weimar Republic was not due solely to the assault by the Nazis, or the impact of the Depression, or the alienation of the middle classes. It was not cut off in its 1924–29 prime. Before 1929 it had already proved highly vulnerable to anti-democratic forces. These were given the chance, by the economic crisis of 1929–33, to do what they had always intended – to bring about the collapse of the parliamentary system. The Reichstag tried to resist the onslaught. But the moderate parties were no match for an authoritarian President willing to allow his constitutional powers to be distorted and to be persuaded to put Hitler into power through the back door of political intrigue.

Questions

1. Was the Weimar Republic 'doomed' to collapse?
2. 'The slide to authoritarian dictatorship after 1930 was inevitable; the appointment of Hitler in 1933 was not.' Do you agree?

ANALYSIS (2): WHAT WERE THE ALTERNATIVES TO THE REPLACEMENT OF THE WEIMAR REPUBLIC BY A NAZI REGIME? WHY DID THESE NOT OCCUR?

By March 1933, Hitler had secured permanent use of the decree law as an alternative to parliamentary legislation; by July he had destroyed the opposition. In 1934 he became Head of State and accelerated the implementation of totalitarian dictatorship through the police state, by mobilising youth and the workforce and by systematic indoctrination, propaganda and persecution. All this was a major departure from the starting point of 30 January 1933: his appointment as Reich Chancellor subject to the authority of the Reich President. Was there no alternative to this slide into totalitarianism? Logic suggests that there were in fact three. One was the return to parliamentary party politics; a second was the continuation of authoritarian dictatorship of the type which had become increasingly apparent since 1930; and the third was a Communist revolution such as that tried in 1919.

There were some signs that parliamentary democracy might revive. The Reichstag attempted on several occasions to take back the initiative from the President by challenging the executive use of Article 48 to bypass the normal legislative process. These votes of no confidence could be countered only by the President dissolving the Reichstag and calling an election. It is also significant that two of the moderate parties who had played a part in earlier coalitions continued to hold their own against the prevailing swing to the right. The Centre Party, for example, actually increased its support from 62 seats in 1928 to 68 in 1930, 75 in July 1932 and 70 in November 1932. The corresponding figures for the SPD were 153, 143, 133 and 121. The Centre Party were, of course, in government between 1930 and 1932 and, irrespective of the personal views held by Brüning, it was not within their tradition to favour any form of dictatorship. Of further promise for the future was the continuing partnership between the Centre Party and SPD in the government of Prussia, showing that coalition and consensus were by no means dead.

But the simple fact is that parliamentary democracy did not reappear. This was largely because the offensive of the right had demolished any chance of the lukewarm and half-hearted coalitions which had been the pattern of the 1920s. After 1930 the only effective channel would have been a broad moderate front determined to sustain a government without presidential support. For a number of reasons this was never a possibility. Parties were still inclined to pursue their own limited interests; the moderating influence of the two liberal parties disintegrated along with the defection of their electoral support to the Nazis; and, above all, President Hindenburg made no effort to restore the influence of the Reichstag. The parties were therefore in the invidious position of having to challenge the President for the rightful application of the Constitution which he was supposed to be upholding, and the President held sufficient power to frustrate that challenge.

Why, then, did Germany not evolve into an authoritarian dictatorship? The conservative right had the advantage of controlling the instruments of power from 1930 onwards. The President sympathised with attempts to weaken the Reichstag and reduce the role of party politics. He made full use of Article 48 to govern by decree and could slap down any attempts by the Reichstag to regain the initiative. The conservative right was also benefiting from the partial decline of parliamentary parties, especially from the collapse of the DDP and DVP. The crisis of confidence in the Weimar Republic seemed to prepare the way logically for a more permanent paternalistic and authoritarian dictatorship. There were examples of this being sustained elsewhere – for example in Austria under Dollfuss and then Schuschnigg. Why therefore should it not have continued indefinitely in Germany?

One reason is that the conservatives changed the whole scenario by enlisting the support of the NSDAP. As we have already seen, the assumption was that the NSDAP was in the process of evolving out of the party form and would eventually join with the DNVP, industry and the army in a broad coalition of right-wing forces. This can, of course, be seen as a miscalculation. The conservative right assumed that they would be able to control Hitler, especially since the electoral performance of the Nazis had dipped in November 1932 by comparison with its showing in July. Had this decision not been taken, the continuation of authoritarian dictatorship could be seen as a valid long-term alternative to the emergence of a totalitarian regime from it. The drift to authoritarian dictatorship and the rise of Hitler were separate processes: what brought them together was an error of judgement.

There is, however, another perspective, which weakens the case for prolonged authoritarianism. Where could the authoritarian presidency have led in the longer term? It seemed to be based essentially on a state of emergency: maintaining this indefinitely would inevitably have created a different type of regime, but it is doubtful that Hindenburg would have wanted to take the initiative here. Although no friend to democracy, he was always punctilious in observing the letter of the Constitution, if not its spirit. Hence he observed Article 25 in calling an election within 60 days of any dissolution carried out to negate the Reichstag's protest against his use of Article 48. But the constitutional use of emergency measures had clearly reached saturation point by January 1933. The appointment of Hitler was offered by Papen as a way out of Hindenburg's difficulty: Hindenburg took it as an alternative to yet another dissolution, this time at the request of Schleicher. It seemed therefore that any continuation of an authoritarian regime would have had to go into a new stage involving perhaps a change in the constitution. The form this would have taken is debatable but would probably have meant the replacement of party politics along the lines of the broad patriotic fronts proposed by right-wing theorists like Zehrer. (8) It is therefore unlikely that conservative dictatorship could have stood still; nor could it have gone backwards in to the days of the Second Reich. This meant that the conservative right's merger with Nazism was not so much an aberration as a logical part of its search for a new identity.

The third main possibility – and the alternative to constitutional revival and permanent authoritarianism – was a Communist revolution. There were certain circumstances which objectively seemed to favour this. The crisis of the Depression seemed to suggest that capitalism was fundamentally threatened and that Germany could experience the revolution that eluded it in 1919. And why not? The Spartacist failure was thus no more ridiculous than the failure of the Munich Putsch four years later. The KPD increased its support more rapidly than the NSDP in the 1920s and its leadership became increasingly confident that revolution would ultimately succeed. Thälmann was certain that the Depression would radicalise the working class, and pull their vote, in much the same way as the Nazis were affecting the middle classes. The KPD would cause the collapse of the SPD in much the same way as the NSDAP had dismantled the liberal parties. Even if Hitler did come to power, there were certain advantages. The NSDAP would shake the bourgeois system to its foundations and would, in turn, soon be overthrown by a genuine proletarian revolution. By this perspective, Nazism was little more than the crude precursor to Communism.

Why did this not happen? It is true that the KPD did increase their representation in the Reichstag from 54 in 1928 to 77 in 1930, 89 in July 1932 and 100 in November 1932. They were, however, never able to become a mass party in the sense that the Nazis were. This was because there was no Communist counterpart to the Nazi rise from the ruins of other parties. Although they did lose part of their support, the SPD did not collapse. Instead, they continued to compete aggressively with the KPD to retain the support of the working class which was, after all, their main constituency. They saw the KPD as potentially even more dangerous than the right and, when Papen took over the Prussian government from them in 1932, they avoided calling a general strike in case this would benefit the Communists. Nor did the KPD have the equivalent of the helping hand given to the Nazis by the DNVP. They therefore had no bridge between their own radicalism and the other sectors of the German population – no short cut to electoral respectability.

Finally, the KPD had no counterpart to the personal charisma of Hitler; nor did they have any of his reorganisational skills. The Communists did, like the Nazis, change their approach to power after the failure of the first attempt at revolution. They were prepared to contest elections to the Reichstag and, if necessary, use legal means to achieve power. But they did not have the means of delivering the rest of the strategy. If anything, they were directly impeded by the intervention of an outside agency which, of course, the Nazis lacked. The KPD looked for its ultimate guidance to Stalin, even though his strategy was geared to the needs of the Soviet Union and was not really in the interests of the German Communist Party at all. His aim was to serve Soviet foreign policy by helping to provoke conflict between Germany and the western capitalist states, with the Soviet Union becoming involved when these had fought each other to the point of exhaustion. It therefore suited his interests to have Hitler in power.

This can be seen as the left-wing equivalent to the blunder of the conservative right. Assisted by such willing accomplices as conservatism and Communism, it is not difficult to see why Nazism was the eventual beneficiary of the collapse of Weimar democracy.

Questions

1. Did the forces for democracy 'give up' after 1930?
2. Why did Germany fall to Nazism rather than Communism in 1933?
3. Did Hitler's dictatorship arise naturally out of Hindenburg's?

SOURCES

1. PROPAGANDA FOR ELECTORAL SUPPORT

Source A: An election poster produced by the NSDAP in 1932.

[See Figure 4, page 104]

Source B: An election poster produced by the SPD in 1932.

[See Figure 5, page 105]

Source C: An election poster produced by the Centre Party.

[See Figure 6, page 106]

Source D: An election poster produced by the NSDAP.

[See Figure 7, page 107]

Source E: A cartoon by John Heartfield, produced in 1932.

[See Figure 8, page 108]

**Figure 4   An election poster produced by the NSDAP in 1932
(*Our Last Hope: HITLER*).**
Source: AKG (London).

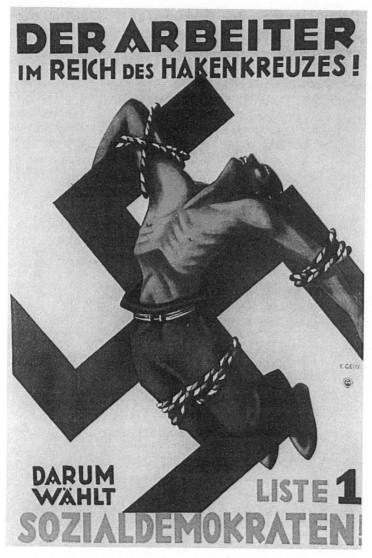

Figure 5   An election poster produced by the SPD in 1932
(*'The worker in the Empire of the Swastika! Therefore vote for the Social Democrats! (List 1)'*)
Source: Süddeutscher Verlag.

Source C

Figure 6   An election poster produced by the Centre Party ('Women and men, ensure the happiness of your family and children by voting for the Christian People's Party').
Source: Hoover Institution Archives.

Figure 7   An election poster produced by the NSDAP (*'NSDAP People's Community. If you need advice and help turn to your local group'*)
Source: Wiener Library.

Figure 8 A cartoon by John Heartfield, produced in 1932 (*The real meaning of the Hitler salute: A small man asking for big gifts. Motto: Millions stand behind me!*).

Source: Akademie der Kunste.

Questions

1. How effectively do Sources A and B present their appeal to the workforce?
2. What are the similarities and differences between the handling of the family theme in Sources C and D?
   How would you explain these?
*3. How accurate is Source E as a representation of the rise of the Nazis?

Worked answer

*3. The Heartfield cartoon converts Hitler's characteristically idio-syncratic salute into a backhander, in receipt of money from a looming figure representing big business. Heartfield was the most perceptive and brilliant cartoonist of the Weimar Republic and this is perhaps his best-known work. It comments on the close relationship between the NSDAP and the major industrialists, such as Thyssen, and the leaders of cartels like I.G. Farben. It could also indicate the close connection with the DNVP which enabled the funds of Hugenberg's party to assist Nazi publicity. The figure in the background could also be the embodiment of the unity of the right shown in the Harzburg Front.

On the other hand, the cartoon is not merely a commentary. Heartfield was a Communist and would therefore be showing the stereotyped image of the dependence of the right on the forces of capitalism – of which fascism was seen typically as the ultimate stage. The cartoon is therefore a strongly polemical image and can also be seen as a piece of party propaganda.

SOURCES

2. THE POLITICAL CRISIS, 1932–33

Source F: Declaration of the SPD anti-Fascist front to the KPD in Vorwärts, 18 June 1932.

. . . A unification of the proletariat is more essential than ever before. The fascist danger demands this unity. The danger of fascism however can only be countered when a genuine common will to unity is present . . .

But you have made it impossible to pursue the necessary united front against fascism because of your year-long attempts to subvert and dismember strong workers' organisations, your common cause with the fascists both inside and outside parliament, your attempts to cripple the Trade Union movement through the Revolutionary Trade Unions, and your slogans . . . 'Social Democracy – the real enemy'.

Source G: from a memorandum by the Reich Minister of the Interior, following the election of July 1932.

Looked at politically, objectively, the result of the election is so fearful because it seems clear that the present election will be the last normal Reichstag election for a long time to come . . . The elected Reichstag is totally incapable of functioning . . .

The one consolation could be the recognition that the National Socialists have passed their peak, since, in comparison with the Prussian elections, they have declined in most constituencies, but against this stands the fact that the radicalism of the right has unleashed a strong radicalism on the left. The communists have made gains almost everywhere and these internal political disturbances have become exceptionally bitter. If things are faced squarely and soberly the situation is such that more than half the German people have declared themselves against the present state, but have not said what sort of state they would accept. Thus any organic development is for the moment impossible. As the lesser of many evils to be feared . . . would be the open assumption of dictatorship by the present government.

Source H: A report from *Kölnische Zeitung*, 28 January 1933.

Reich Chancellor von Schleicher today informed the Reich President about the situation. He declared that the present Reich government would be unable to defend itself *vis-à-vis* the Reichstag if it did not obtain in advance the power to dissolve parliament. The Reich President von Hindenburg stated that he could not grant this proposal because of current conditions. Reich Chancellor von Schleicher then announced the resignation of the government since it had lost the confidence of the Reich President and therefore could not continue in office . . . Reich President von Hindenburg summoned former Reich Chancellor von Papen and requested him to clarify the political situation and to suggest possible political procedures.

Questions

1. What was the KPD (Source F)? [1]
   Explain the reference to 'Prussian elections' (Source G). [2]

2. How useful is Source G to the historian studying the movement towards dictatorship in Germany? [4]

*3. How accurate is Source H as a record of the fall of the von Schleicher government? [6]

4. Compare the language and tone of Sources G and H. [5]

5. To what extent does Source F bear out the assertion in Source G that 'the radicalism of the right has unleashed a strong radicalism on the left'? Use your own knowledge to explain any inconsistency between the two sources. [7]

Worked answer

*3. [The answer to this question will certainly need additional knowledge, which should be used not only to supplement the source but also to show that the source is misleading.]

Source H provides the barest outline of the events leading to the fall of Schleicher's government. It was based upon an official government release to the press and therefore would not have given any indication of the reasons for the fall. The *Kölnische Zeitung* offered no speculation or reflection on these. This suggests that the resignation came as a surprise and that the background to it was kept secret. The report therefore contained no reference to the intrigues between Papen and Hitler to bring about Schleicher's fall.

A retrospective knowledge of these intrigues shows just how bland and misleading the report is. The inability of 'the present Reich government would be unable to defend itself *vis-à-vis* the Reichstag' was due to the agreement between Hitler and Papen that the NSDAP should join the votes of no confidence against von Schleicher's use of decree laws under Article 48. The refusal of Hindenburg to grant Schleicher's request for a dissolution 'because of current conditions' suggests that the President felt he could not keep resorting to this prerogative, especially since Papen had already proposed to him the alternative of a coalition led by Hitler. This was the real reason for Hindenburg summoning Papen 'to clarify the political situation' and to suggest 'possible political procedures'.

8

SOCIAL AND CULTURAL ACHIEVEMENTS

BACKGROUND NARRATIVE

Much of this book has focused on the political and economic problems and achievements of the Weimar Republic. This final chapter looks at the social and cultural developments in a period renowned for the changes experienced by the German people.

ANALYSIS (1): HOW EXTENSIVE WERE THE SOCIAL ACHIEVEMENTS OF THE WEIMAR REPUBLIC?

The Weimar Republic is usually seen as an interlude of social change between the more repressive periods of the Second and Third Reichs. To an extent, this is true. There were examples of remarkable progress in defining individual liberties and obligations and in setting up an advanced welfare state, while certain groups within society were emancipated from some of the constraints and stigmas previously attached to them. There are, however, two qualifications to this overall view. One is that some of the precedents had already been evident before 1914 in Wilhelmine Germany. The other is that the social achievements of the Weimar Republic were never sufficient to win the political allegiance of the majority of the population or to prevent a substantial proportion from voting for the more repressive social solutions offered by the parties of the right and the far left.

The Weimar Republic had the most explicit statement of civil rights ever produced in a constitutional document. Germans were guaranteed 'equality before the law' (Article 109) and 'liberty of travel and residence' (Article 111). Their 'personal liberty' was 'inviolable' (Article 114), while 'the house of every German' was 'his sanctuary' (Article 115). In addition, each individual had 'the right . . . to express his opinion freely by word, in writing, in print, in picture form, or in any other way' (Article 118): indeed, censorship was 'forbidden' (Article 142). (1) On the other hand, these articles were diluted by provisions that permitted 'exceptions . . . by authority of law'. The effect of the guarantees was nullified whenever Article 48 came into use. Social and intellectual freedoms could therefore be interpreted politically – a fundamental contradiction with dangerous implications.

The Weimar Republic produced probably the most advanced welfare state in the western world. Again, specific commitments were to be seen in the Constitution. By Article 151, for example, 'The regulation of economic life must be compatible with the principles of justice, with the aim of attaining humane conditions of existence for all', while, under Article 161, 'The Reich shall organize a comprehensive system of [social] insurance'. (2) The Constitution also contained a commitment to full employment and to the creation of a positive working environment: by Article 165 'Workers and employees are called upon to cooperate, on an equal footing, with employers in the regulation of wages and of the conditions of labour'. (3) Altogether, this was an impressive undertaking. Yet it was not entirely innovatory. The basis of social security had already been introduced during the Second Reich. For example, a series of laws from 1881 onwards had established a rudimentary system, which was further developed by the Reich Insurance Order of 1911. What happened in the Weimar Republic was not, therefore, a new departure in terms of principle but rather a huge step in scope. On the other hand, these developments were fundamentally flawed. There was a growing gap between the intervention by the government on the one hand and the influence of the great industrial cartels on the other. Government policy was to increase welfare benefits and allow for a steady rise in wages while, at the same time, intervening where possible to limit the damage caused by industrial disputes and to impose arbitration procedures. The industrialists, meanwhile, became increasingly concerned about the prospect of what they saw as a rebellious workforce standing too firmly on its guaranteed rights. Welfare policies were increasingly attacked by the cartels as undermining the process of industrial recovery. One of the reasons why industrial leaders swung sharply to the right was their desire to see within Germany a disciplined workforce. Expenditure on the welfare services was financed largely by the loans secured by Germany as a result of the Dawes Plan. The whole social infrastructure of Weimar was therefore insecure and began to come apart as a result of the withdrawal of investments after 1929. During boom years the welfare system worked and could be financed, but when the boom turned into depression the welfare state could not cope. There was a particularly strong backlash. Public expectations of the state were greatly increased, which made the Republic more vulnerable to desertion in times of crisis when the economic situation forced it to cut back on welfare provision. Social provision therefore failed to secure a consistent base of political support.

One social group stood to gain a great deal from the Republic. Women experienced considerable social and economic advancement, partly from the more progressive and egalitarian climate of the Republic and partly from the specific guarantees within its Constitution. By Article 109, for example, 'Men and women have the same fundamental civil rights and duties'. (4) The results were impressive: the election of 111 women to the Reichstag in 1920 and a higher degree of representation within the professions. The more liberal atmosphere also saw the emergence of sexual politics in the form of the League for the Protection of Mothers (BFM), which demanded free abortion and government financial assistance to unmarried mothers. Fashion was a further factor: the relative prosperity of the period after 1923 encouraged women to wear more adventurous styles. On the other hand, the process of emancipation was by no means complete. There was strong resistance within most parties to the complete implementation of equal rights. This was to be expected from the right but was to be found even within the left, which tended to submerge this issue into that of working conditions and political activism. Hence the SPD opposed equal pay and the KPD tended to see women as an adjunct to the male-dominated revolutionary movement. Among women themselves were movements which opposed any fundamental change. The League of German Women's Associations (BDF) emphasised women's role as moral reformers in society. Overall, the role of women during the Republic was ambivalent and there was a confusion of identity which led many to support the parties emphasising traditional roles and security. Initially this meant the DNVP, later the NSDAP. Either way, the Republic promised much to women but never really convinced them that it could deliver.

Another group which should have benefited greatly was the Jews. In theory, Weimar gave them more opportunities for self-fulfilment and equality with other Germans than any previous regime. There was certainly a considerable Jewish participation in the transition from the

Second Reich to the Republic: after all, the Constitution was drafted by a Jewish lawyer, Hugo Preuss. They also contributed a great deal to the intellectual achievements of the period, the best-known example being the writer Arnold Zweig. Nevertheless, the condition of the Jews did not improve uniformly. There were still underlying trends of anti-Semitism, associated especially with the conservative and radical right. Jews were sufficiently alarmed about this to establish organisations to try to convince the population of their valid contributions to Germany. Two examples were the Fatherland Association of Jewish Front Soldiers, intended to publicise the patriotism of Jews during the First World War, and the Central Association of German Citizens of the Jewish Faith. Particularly menacing to the Jews was the Nazi propaganda against them. Hitler saw anti-Semitism as one of the key issues of the NSDAP's programme and as a means of cutting through class differences to reconcile Germans of different social origins to a common cause. Thus the darker legacy of the Second Reich was strengthened by the incipient Third Reich to prevent the more tolerant policies of the Republic from having any permanent effect.

To what extent did Weimar enhance the conditions and prospects of the various social classes? The upper classes, who had tried to perpetuate their dominance in the Second Reich, had no reason to celebrate the egalitarian nature of the Weimar Constitution, which specifically abolished 'legal privileges or disadvantages of birth or of rank' as well as 'titles of nobility' and 'orders and decorations'. (5) Many therefore supported the DNVP, with some of the agricultural interest later moving over to the NSDAP. The middle classes, it might be thought, would have benefited more from a system which was intended to be progressive and to reward enterprise. At first this held true, with the majority of the middle-class vote going to the DVP, Centre Party and DDP. Unfortunately, this section of the population was particularly susceptible to economic crisis of the very type over which the Republic had so little direct control. The newer middle class, in particular, fell victim to circumstances. This consisted of employees in the new service industries as well as in business and administration who felt trapped between large-scale capitalism at one extreme and the labour interests at the other. These were accentuated by the rationalisation of the economy during the period of the Republic and the development of scientific management and the growth of cartels. Feeling threatened by such developments, the new middle class proved exceptionally susceptible to the appeal of the Nazis. The process was already beginning before 1929 but was greatly aggravated by the onset of the Great Depression.

The working class had most to gain from the Republic – and therefore most to lose from its destruction. This is shown by the consistency of their support for the SPD after 1930 at the time when the middle classes were deserting the liberal parties for the NSDAP. Clearly they valued the welfare state, the right to full trade union powers, the steady increase in wages during the 1920s and the replacement of the social elitism of the Second Reich with an egalitarian ethos. Nevertheless, a growing minority were drawn into support for the revolutionary far left. This was a strong indication of disillusionment with the limitations of the Republic. Egalitarianism was not accompanied by the proletarianisation demanded by the KPD: the radicals therefore saw the Republic as merely an alternative form of bourgeois rule to the Second Reich. There was no workers' control in industry, no state enterprises, no 'people's army': all these had died with the collapse of the Spartacist uprising. Instead, there was continued control by the conservative forces over law and order, the judiciary and, above all, the Reichswehr. To a resentful upper class and a volatile middle class we must therefore add a deeply divided working class.

The underlying problem of the Weimar Republic was that it failed to satisfy more than a minority of social aspirations. Some groups and sectional interests were permanently alienated. Others had their expectations raised, only to find that the economic and political base of the Republic was not equal to the task of sustaining them. The result was disillusionment – and therefore alienation. This does not necessarily reduce the scope of the initial achievement but it does show how vulnerable that achievement was.

Questions

1. Was social change under the Weimar Republic an 'illusion'?
2. Did the Weimar Republic achieve more in terms of social change than it did politically or economically?

ANALYSIS (2): DID THE WEIMAR REPUBLIC SEE A 'GOLDEN AGE OF GERMAN CULTURE'?

As with any other issue concerning the Weimar Republic, the developments in culture have been the subject of considerable controversy, both contemporary and recent.

One view is that the Weimar Republic was culturally one of the most creative periods in German history, therefore warranting its designation as a 'golden age'. Certainly there was an impressive array of endeavour which escaped confinement to any one of the arts and spread across them all. The key painters of the time produced a variety of ideas and techniques. Some, like George Grosz, used the medium to criticise society: his *Grey Day* comments on the boredom experienced by most people in their everyday lives. Others were members of new movements. Hannah Hoech, for example, was one of the Dada School, which believed that the absurd should be considered normal. Much of her work was in the form of collage, assembled from smaller items, including photographs. Architecture and design were also profoundly affected by the new Bauhaus movement of Walter Gropius (1883–1969). Germany also became the centre for new plays and operas. The most famous playwright of the time was Bertolt Brecht, whose *Three-penny Opera* was an enormous success. Films were also experimental: *The Cabinet of Dr Calgari* was publicised as a horror film, but its real message was anti-military and anti-war. Literature was dominated by Arnold Zweig, Hermann Hesse, Stefan George, Thomas Mann and Erich Remarque. The last of these wrote the celebrated anti-war novel, *All Quiet on the Western Front*. Perhaps the greatest changes were seen in music: Arnold Schoenberg and Alban Berg developed 'tonal' music, or music which emphasised notes rather than melody or 'tunes'. In general, lively debate flourished in the atmosphere of completely free expression allowed by the Republic. At the centre of this hectic activity was Berlin, with its 120 newspapers and periodicals and 40 theatres. Thomas Mann claimed with some justification that Germany had replaced France as the cultural centre of Europe. He might also have added that Berlin had replaced Paris.

There have, however, been criticisms of this approach. These have come from two directions. First, even if we accept that these achievements were remarkable (which is in itself debatable), should the Weimar Republic receive all the credit for them? It can just as readily be argued that the main impetus came from the Second Reich and that the Weimar brought to maturity what had already been growing; or, in the words of Peter Gay, 'the Republic created little; it liberated what was already there.' (6) But this seems to dismiss the achievements of the Republic too lightly. It is true that cultural experimentation did exist before the First World War, especially in the form of expressionism. Nevertheless, the authoritarian Second Reich was fundamentally unsympathetic to such developments and it was the more liberal atmosphere provided by the Weimar Republic which really enabled the arts to flourish. The Revolution of 1918 swept away the conservative constraints and initially promoted a cultural form which reflected the political ferment. Gradually, however, cultural experimentation became more secure, establishing itself during the 1920s as convention.

The development of architecture is a typical example of this trend. Modern architecture was a pre-war phenomenon, the German Werkbund of architects and designers having been set up by Hermann Muthesius in 1907. This was already experimenting with steel and glass and rejecting some of the more ponderous conventions of the nineteenth century which seemed to have affected Britain and Germany in equal proportions. Hence the Weimar Republic did not create anew. Nevertheless, the First World War did have a major impact on architectural styles. Initially these were politicised to the extent of reflecting revolution. The early products of this were highly original, including Mendelsohn's Einstein Observatory, completed in 1921. The process then settled down into a more formal trend but continued to influence the whole of the Weimar period with its use of coloured glass, concrete and painted walls.

The second criticism of the Weimar Republic's 'golden age' is more fundamental; the notion that there was any cultural resurgence is fatally flawed. The new developments by no means elicited the support of all artists or writers. In fact, many directly rejected it and substantial sections of the population were also indifferent to the changes. The hostility became increasingly politicised, emanating from the Communist left and the far right.

Communists believed that the *new* style was decadent and bourgeois, introspective and trivial: it had nothing to do with mobilising proletarian revolutionary feeling and commitment, which was the real purpose of art. Experimentation for its own sake was a luxury and did not reflect the real needs of the working class. The conservative and radical right, ironically, saw the cultural changes as inspired by the influences of Communism and therefore as a fundamental threat to Germany's national health. Critics like Wilhelm Stapel feared that the 'cesspool of the Republic' would pollute all that was 'noble and healthy'. (7) Both the Nazi Party and the DNVP considered that what was being produced in the Weimar Republic was 'decadent' and unpatriotic, seeking to trivialise and choosing deliberately to ignore Germany's traditional virtues. Between the two extremes were many ordinary people in Germany who were confused by the rapid changes in culture. They were not impressed when they heard Schoenberg's music at concerts or saw the new buildings or furniture of Gropius. Many also blamed the new wave of art for a decline of moral standards in the 1920s. Berlin had a huge number of night-clubs and there was more emphasis on sex in entertainment even than in Paris. Some people reacted prudishly to this, others were genuinely worried.

German criticism of Weimar culture was much stronger than, for example, French criticism of the culture of the Third Republic before 1914. This does not, however, invalidate the view that there was a 'golden age' – certainly when compared with the nightmarish philis- tinism of the Third Reich which consigned the works of Weimar to the 'museums of degenerate art'. The liberal atmosphere of the Republic encouraged the fulfilment of trends already started during the Second Reich and its achievements were acknowledged throughout Europe. Unfortunately, the Republic did not receive popular political loyalty in return. The only direct relationship between culture and politics existed among the opponents of the Republic: cultural and political con- servatism combined far more effectively than cultural and political liberalism. Ultimately, therefore, the Republic's 'golden age' had no political equivalent; cultural achievement did not translate into political stability.

Questions

1. Is the 'golden age' an accurate concept when applied to the culture of the Weimar Republic?
2. 'During the period of the Weimar Republic, the effects of cultural experimentation were basically negative.' Is this true?

SOURCES

1. THE WEIMAR REPUBLIC AND WOMEN

Source A: *Manifesto for International Women's Day*, 25 March 1921.

TO ALL WORKING WOMEN!

Working women, employed women of all kinds in city and countryside, small property-holders, mothers of the proletariat and the dispossessed.

Come out for International Women's Day!
It must become your day!

Your lives and deeds are dominated by exorbitant price increases with which small and medium incomes cannot keep pace. Exorbitant prices deplete your bread and season it with the bitterest of worries and scalding tears. They tear the shirt from the backs of your children and rob them of their rosy cheeks and happy smiles. Uncounted numbers of you are massed in stifling back rooms, in dark and airless courtyard apartments, in damp, mouldy cellars and draughty garrets. Unmanageable fees and taxes increase the burden of your worries and add to your privations.

. . . The house they talk about, what is it? The exploitative capitalist economy transforms it from a home – a place of rest, peace, and happiness – into a treadmill whose operation mercilessly crushes you, body and soul.

. . . The women communists . . . in Russia are taking the lead, setting an example for the women struggling here. The revolution in Russia is also their immortal work. With it demands for rights were fulfilled for which women in other countries must still struggle hard. Your Women's Day can call the manual and mental labourers to work on the construction of the communist order.

Source B: from an article by Alfred Polgar, 1928: *A Conversation between Men*.

My son, I noted with some discomfort that you kept your seat on the streetcar, instead of offering it to one of the women who otherwise must stand. Does it count as modern to be a boor?

Father, you have slept through some new developments. The women of your time acknowledged their weaknesses as a claim to all manner of protection and consideration, as the weak are owed by the strong. This obligation grew out of the circumstance that they didn't share the rights that men had . . . That has changed. It was the women themselves, due to an easily understood hunger for air and life, who shattered the bell jar in which they were vegetating. They have become comrades in work and play, in pleasure and struggle, and among comrades everything is equal.

Source C: from *Back to the Good Old Days* by Alice Ruhle-Gerstel, an article published in January 1933.

This new figure never became average, never became the mass female. There was no time for that. Until today this new figure has remained a pioneer, the standard bearer . . . that had yet to develop. But before she could evolve into a type and expand into an average, she once again ran up against barriers. Her old womanly fate – motherhood, love, family – trailed after her into the spheres of the new womanliness, which immediately presented itself as a new objectivity. And she therefore found herself not liberated, as she had naively assumed, but now doubly bound: conflicts between work and marriage now appeared, between uninhibited drives and inhibited mores, conflicts between the public and private aspects of her life, which could not be synthesized . . . It easily appeared as if the new freedom for women had achieved nothing.

Source D: from *Twilight for Women?*, an article published on 7 July 1931.

Women have become unpopular. That is not good news because it touches on things that cannot be explained by reason alone. An uncomfortable atmosphere is gathering around all working women. A perhaps unorganized but very powerful countermovement is taking place at all of them . . .

Along the entire spectrum from left to right the meaning of women's employment and their right to it are suddenly being questioned, more or less directly. At the moment it is not even the old discussion over so-called 'equal rights', over 'equal pay for equal work' that occupies the foreground. Suddenly we are obliged to counter the most primitive arguments against the gainful employment of women.

Source E: from a Nazi leaflet issued during the Reichstag election campaign, July 1932.

GERMAN WOMEN! GERMAN WOMEN! GERMAN MOTHERS! GERMAN MOTHERS!

Our Young People Defiled:
. . . This is a result of the many years during which our people, and in particular our youth, have been exposed to a flood of muck and filth, in word and print, in the theatre and in the cinema. These are the results of the systematic Marxist destruction of the family . . .

. . . Is there no possibility of salvation? Must our people, our youth, sink without hope of rescue into the muck and filth? No!!! The National Socialists must win the election so that they can put a halt to this Marxist handiwork, so that once again women are honoured and valued, and so that the cinema and theatre contributes to the inner rebuilding of the nation.

German women and mothers. Do you want your honour to sink still further? Do you want your daughters to be playthings and the objects of sexual lust? If NOT then vote for a National Socialist Majority on JULY 31st.

Questions

1. Explain the reference to 'this Marxist handiwork' (Source E). [2]
2. How might the author of Source C have reacted to the two points of view in Source B? [5]
3. Sources C and D are largely similar. But in what ways do they differ? [5]
4. Are both Sources A and E merely propaganda? [5]
5. 'The Weimar Republic achieved nothing for women.' Using Sources A to E, and your own knowledge, do you agree with this view? [8]

NOTES

1. THE GERMAN REVOLUTION, 1918–19

1 L.L. Snyder: *The Weimar Republic* (Princeton, NJ 1966), p. 22.
2 Ibid., p. 23.
3 H. Wehler: *The German Empire 1871–1918* (trans 1985, Providence, RI), p. 229.
4 P. Bookbinder: *Weimar Germany* (Manchester 1996), p. 30.
5 E. Kolb: *The Weimar Republic* (trans P.S. Falla, London 1988), p. 141.
6 V.R. Berghahn: *Modern Germany: Society, Economy and Politics in the Twentieth Century* (Cambridge 1987), p. 63.
7 E. Kolb: op. cit., p. 16.
8 J.W. Hiden: *Republican and Fascist Germany* (London 1996), p. 8.
9 L.L. Snyder: op. cit., p. 137. Reading No. 18: The Weimar Constitution.
10 H. Heiber: *The Weimar Republic* (trans W.E. Yuill, Oxford 1993), p. 12.
11 J.W. Hiden: *The Weimar Republic* (Harlow 1974), p. 3.
Source A: A. Kaes, M. Jay and E. Dimendberg, eds: *The Weimar Republic Sourcebook* (Berkeley 1994), pp. 88–9.
Source B: Ibid., pp. 96–100.
Source C: Ibid., pp. 56–8.
Source D: Philip Scheidemann: *The Making of the New Germany: Memoirs*, trans. J.E. Michell (New York 1929), II, pp. 261–3.
Source E: *The New York Times*, November 29, 1918.
Source F: J. Laver: *Imperial and Weimar Germany* (London 1992), pp. 40–1.
Source G: Ibid., pp. 39–40.

2. THE CONSTITUTION AND POLITICAL SYSTEM

1 L.L. Snyder: op. cit.; Reading No. 18: The Weimar Constitution.
2 Ibid.
3 Ibid.
4 P. Bookbinder: op. cit., p. 52.
5 See H. Boldt: 'Article 48 of the Weimar Constitution, its historical and political implications', in A Nicholls, ed.: *German Democracy and the Triumph of Hitler: Essays in Recent German History* (London 1971).
6 E. Eyck: *A History of the Weimar Republic* (Cambridge, MA. 1962), Vol. 1, Ch. 10.
7 H. Heiber: op. cit., p. 132,
8 K.D. Bracher: *The German Dictatorship* (Harmondsworth 1973), p. 218.
9 M. Broszat: *The Hitler State: The Foundation and Development of the Internal Structure of the Third Reich* (trans J.W. Hiden, London 1981), p. 11.
10 E. Fraenkel: 'Historical handicaps of German parliamentarianism', in *The Road to Dictatorship 1918-1933* (London 1970).
11 J.W. Hiden: *Republican and Fascist Germany*, p. 51.
12 J.W. Hiden: *The Weimar Republic*, p. 21.
13 P. Bookbinder: op. cit., p. 47.
14 H. Mommsen: 'Government without parties. Conservative plans for constitutional revision at the end of the Weimar Republic', in L.E. Jones and J. Retallack, eds: *Between Reform Reaction and Resistance: Studies in the History of German Conservatism from 1789 to 1945* (Providence, RI 1993), p. 350.
15 V.R. Berghahn: op. cit., p. 87.
16 M. Broszat: op. cit., p. 2.
17 J.W. Hiden: *Republican and Fascist Germany*, p. 60.
18 H. Mommsen: op. cit., p. 366.
19 Ibid., pp. 366–7.
20 S. Taylor: *Germany 1918–1933* (London 1983), Ch. 4.
Source A: L.L. Snyder: op. cit, pp. 137–43.
Source B: A. Kaes, M. Jay and E. Dimendberg: op. cit., p. 89.
Source C: W.C. Runciman, ed.: *Max Weber, Selections in Translation* (Cambridge 1978), trans. Eric Matthews.
Source D: A. Kaes, M. Jay and E. Dimendberg: op. cit., pp. 110–11.
Sources E and F: Figures adapted from H. Boldt: 'Article 48 of the Weimar Constitution in its historical and political implications', in A. Nicholls, ed.: *German Democracy and the Triumph of Hitler: Essays in Recent German History* (London 1971).
Source G: J. Remak, ed.: *The Nazi Years* (Englewood Cliffs, NJ 1969), p. 21.

Source I: A. Kaes, M. Jay and E. Dimendberg: op. cit., pp. 104–5.
Source J: Ibid., pp. 112–15.
Source K: Ibid. pp. 115–16.

3. VERSAILLES AND ITS IMPACT

1 J. Bariéty: *Les Relations franco-allemande après la première guerre mondiale* (Paris 1977); W.A. McDougall: *France's Rhineland Diplomacy 1914–1924* (Princeton, NJ 1978); S.A. Schuker: *The End of French Predominance in Europe. The Financial Crisis of 1924 and the Adoption of the Dawes Plan* (Chapel Hill, NC 1976); M. Trachtenberg: *Reparations in World Politics: France and European Economic Diplomacy, 1916–1923* (New York 1980).
2 H. Heiber: op. cit., p. 39.
3 See J. Mayer: *Politics and the Diplomacy of Peacemaking. Containment and Counter-Revolution at Versailles 1918–1919* (London 1967).
4 Quoted in E. Kolb: op. cit., p.169.
5 Ibid., p. 170.
Source A: J.A.S. Grenville: *The Major International Treaties 1914– 1973* (London 1974), pp. 59ff.
Source B: Alma Luckau: *The German Delegation at the Paris Peace Conference* (New York 1941).
Source C: *The German White Book Concerning the Responsibility of the Authors of the War* (New York 1924), p. 21.
Source D: Count Max Montgelas: *The Case for the Central Powers* (London 1925), pp. 200–3.

4. CRISIS AND RECOVERY, 1919–23

1 L.L. Snyder: op. cit., Ch. 5.
2 G. Layton: *From Bismarck to Hitler: Germany 1890–1933* (London 1995), p. 93.
3 E. Kolb: op. cit., pp. 40–1.
4 L.L. Snyder: op. cit., p. 55.
5 E. Kolb: op. cit., p. 34.
6 L.L. Snyder: op. cit., p. 63.
Source A: L.L. Snyder: op. cit., Reading No. 19, pp. 144–5.
Source B: Quoted in Harlan R. Crippen, ed.: *Germany: A Self-Portrait* (London 1944), p. 162.
Source C: J. Noakes and G. Pridham, eds *Nazism 1919–1945: A Documentary Reader* (Exeter 1983), Vol. 1, p. 34.
Source D: L.L. Snyder: op. cit., p. 156.

Source E: G. Layton: *From Bismarck to Hitler: Germany 1890–1933* (London 1995), p. 92.

Source F: J Remak: op. cit., p. 23.

Source G: Cited in Bry, G.: *Wages in Germany, 1871–1945* (Princeton, NJ 1960).

Source H: Quoted in F.K. Ringer, ed.: *The German Inflation of 1923* (Oxford 1969).

5. A PERIOD OF STABILITY, 1924–29?

1   L.L. Snyder: op. cit., p. 66.
2   Ibid., p. 143.
3   P. Bookbinder: op. cit., p. 169.
4   L.L. Snyder: op. cit., p. 67.
5   D.J.K. Peukert: *The Weimar Republic* (London 1991), p. 122.
6   V.R. Berghahn: op. cit., p. 104.
7   D.J.K. Peukert: op. cit., p. 212.
8   Quoted in D.J.K. Peukert: op. cit., p. 219.
9   E. Kolb: op. cit., p. 67.
10 G. Layton: op. cit., p. 117.

Source A: D.J.K. Peukert: op. cit., pp. 120–1.

Source B: V.R. Berghahn: op. cit., p. 279.

Source C: Ibid., p. 284.

Source D: Ibid., p. 290.

Source E: D.J.K. Peukert: op. cit., pp. 120–1.

Source F: A. Kaes, M. Jay and E. Dimendberg: op. cit., pp. 410–11.

Source H: L.L. Snyder: op. cit., Reading No. 32, pp. 174–5.

Source I: J.W. Hiden: *The Weimar Republic*, document 17, pp. 98–9.

Source J: J. Noakes and G. Pridham: op. cit., p. 50.

6. FOREIGN POLICY

1   J. Laver: *Imperial and Weimar Germany* (London 1992), pp. 59–60.
2   W. Ruge: *Stresemann* (East Berlin 1965), pp. 226, 223.
3   Quoted in V.R. Berghahn: op. cit., p. 99.
4   V.R. Berghahn: op. cit., p. 96.
5   Ibid.
6   Quoted in G. Layton: *From Bismarck to Hitler: Germany 1890–1933* (London 1995), p. 118.
7   Ibid.
8   Ibid.
9   E. Kolb: op. cit., p. 65.

Source A: J. Laver: op. cit., pp. 59–60.
Source B: Eric Sutton, ed. and trans: *Gustav Stresemann: His Diaries, Letters and Papers* (New York 1935–7), II.
Source C: *The League of Nations Official Journal*, Special Supplement No. 44.
Source D: J. Laver: op. cit., pp. 150–1.
Source E: Ibid., pp. 183–4.
Source F: Ibid.: op. cit., pp. 183–4.
Source G: J. Remak: op. cit., p. 109.

7. CRISIS AND COLLAPSE, 1929–33

1 E. Kolb: op. cit., p. 107.
2 W. Conze in ibid., p. 179.
3 F. Meinecke in ibid., p. 179.
4 E. Kolb: op. cit.. Ch. 7.
5 K.D. Bracher in ibid., p. 181.
6 E. Hamburger in ibid., p. 181.
7 Quoted in D.G. Williamson: *The Third Reich* (Harlow 1982), Ch. 3.
8 See H. Mommsen: op. cit.
Source A: AKG London.
Source B: Bilderdienst Süddeutscher Verlag.
Source C: Ibid.
Source D: Wiener Library.
Source E: Akademie der Kunste.
Source F: J. Laver: op. cit., p. 83.
Source G: J.W. Hiden: *The Weimar Republic*, pp. 101–2.
Source H: L.L. Snyder: op. cit., p. 213.

8. SOCIAL AND CULTURAL ACHIEVEMENTS

1 L.L. Snyder: op. cit., Reading No. 18.
2 Ibid.
3 Ibid.
4 Ibid.
5 Ibid.
6 Quoted in V.R. Berghahn: op. cit., p. 83.
7 A. Kaes, M. Jay and E. Dimendberg: op. cit., p. 423.
Source A: A. Kaes, M. Jay and E. Dimendberg: op. cit., pp. 198–9.
Source B: Ibid., p. 204.
Source C: Ibid., p. 218.
Source D: Ibid., p. 210.
Source E: J. Laver: op. cit., pp. 72–3.

BIBLIOGRAPHY

PRIMARY SOURCES

The most comprehensive set of primary sources on the Weimar Republic may be found in A. Kaes, M. Jay and E. Dimendberg, eds: *The Weimar Republic Sourcebook* (Berkeley 1994). More specifically connected with the rise of Hitler is J. Noakes and G. Pridham, eds: *Nazism 1919–1945: A Documentary Reader* (Exeter 1983), Vol. 1. Shorter selections are contained in G.J. Remak, ed.: *The Nazi Years* (Englewood Cliffs, NJ 1969); L.L. Snyder: *The Weimar Republic* (Princeton, NJ 1966) and J.W. Hiden: *The Weimar Republic* (Harlow 1974). Foreign policy is covered in B.H. Nicolson: *Peacemaking 1919* (New York 1939); J.M. Keynes: *The Economic Consequences of the Peace* (London 1919); and E. Grenville, *The Major International Treaties 1914–1973* (London 1974).

SECONDARY SOURCES

One of the most comprehensive works is E. Eyck: *A History of the Weimar Republic* (Cambridge, MA 1962). More recent, and containing a variety of interpretations, are E. Kolb: *The Weimar Republic* (trans P.S. Falla, London 1988); P. Bookbinder: *Weimar Germany* (Manchester 1996); H. Heiber: *The Weimar Republic* (trans W.E. Yuill, Oxford 1993); and V.R. Berghahn: *Modern Germany: Society, Economy and Politics in the Twentieth Century* (Cambridge 1987). Shorter works are J. Hiden: *Republican and Fascist Germany* (London 1996); S. Taylor: *Germany 1918–1933* (London 1983); and G. Layton: *From Bismarck to Hitler: Germany 1890–1933* (London 1995). Collections of essays are contained in A Nicholls, ed.: *German*

Democracy and the Triumph of Hitler: Essays in Recent German History (London 1971); *The Road to Dictatorship 1918–1933* (London 1970); and L.E. Jones and J.. Retallack, eds: *Between Reform Reaction and Resistance: Studies in the History of German Conservatism from 1789 to 1945* (Providence, RI 1993). The connection between Weimar and Nazi Germany is dealt with, although differently, in K.D. Bracher: *The German Dictatorship* (Harmondsworth 1973); and M. Broszat: *The Hitler State: The Foundation and Development of the Internal Structure of the Third Reich* (trans London 1981). Foreign policy is covered by W.A. McDougall: *France's Rhineland Diplomacy 1914–1924* (Princeton, NJ 1978); S.A. Schuker: *The End of French Predominance in Europe. The Financial Crisis of 1924 and the Adoption of the Dawes Plan* (Chapel Hill, NC 1976); M. Trachtenberg: *Reparations in World Politics: France and European Economic Diplomacy, 1916–1923* (New York 1980); and J. Mayer: *Politics and the Diplomacy of Peacemaking. Containment and Counter-Revolution at Versailles 1918–1919* (London 1967).

INDEX